W9-AMW-591

POKER

POKER

BETS, BLUFFS, AND BAD BEATS

A. ALVAREZ

Photo editor, Kelly Duane

CHRONICLE BOOKS

SAN FRANCISCO

First Chronicle Books LLC paperback edition,
published in 2004

Copyright © 2001 by A. Alvarez

All rights reserved. No part of this book
may be reproduced in any form without
written permission from the publisher.

ISBN - 0-8118-4627-X
The Library of Congress has
cataloged the previous edition
as follows:

Alvarez, A. (Alfred), 1929–
Poker: bets, bluffs, and bad beats /
A. Alvarez.
          p.   cm.
ISBN 0-8118-4627-X

1. Poker. I. Title.
GV1251 .A48 2000
795.41'2—dc21
00-057097

Designed by **Jeremy G. Stout**
Typography by Suzanne Scott
Printed in China

An abridged version of "Chapter 7: The
World Series, 1994," originally appeared
in the *New Yorker* on August 8th, 1994,
under the title "No Limit."

Page 127 constitutes a continuation
of the copyright page.

Distributed in Canada by Raincoast Books
9050 Shaughnessy Street
Vancouver, British Columbia V6P 6E5

10 9 8 7 6 5 4 3 2

Chronicle Books LLC
85 Second Street
San Francisco, California 94105

www.chroniclebooks.com

TO CYRUS AND CAROLINE GHANI

"Old poker players never die, they just get bigger pots."

TABLE *of* CONTENTS

INTRODUCTION:
Learning to Play

Is that the game where one receives five cards? And if there's two alike that's pretty good, but if there's three alike that's much better?

W. C. Fields

For the past forty years or more I have played poker regularly once or twice a week, except when I am in Las Vegas, when I play all day every day for a couple of weeks on end. Playing poker is what I like to do with my spare time and what I would prefer to do if I didn't have to work for a living. Other people feel the same about golf or chess or line dancing, but what I am talking about here is something more than an absorbing pastime. Poker changed my life, and sometimes I think it may even have saved it.

Yet I still can't figure out how I ever came to play the game. After all, I'm an Englishman and, until recently, poker was not much played in England—certainly not by my family. When I was young there were ill-tempered bridge games at home every Sunday: my parents versus my domineering grandfather and a gloomy widowed neighbor named Doris, whom my father nicknamed Black Bess because she always dressed in black and seemed to be in permanent mourning for her henpecked late husband. My parents were dreadful bridge players, and the Sunday games

created so much bad blood that I vowed never to learn. Card games, I decided, had nothing to do with pleasure; they were an institutionalized excuse for squabbling, like marriage.

Added to that, I don't believe in luck, and, although I have been addicted to risk all my life—rock climbing, high-board diving, fast cars—I don't much like gambling. Roulette, craps, slot machines, and similar games of chance leave me cold. In 1981, for example, I spent three long weeks at the old Golden Nugget in downtown Las Vegas. I played poker every day but never placed a single dollar bet on the roulette table or put a quarter in a slot, despite the fact that the Golden Nugget, in those days, was so cunningly constructed that it was impossible to go out onto the street without passing through the casino. As for horses, the only time I ever backed a winner, the race was declared void.

But poker isn't about gambling, although I didn't know that when I started playing. Like all beginners, I thought poker was a game of pure chance, like

⊗ Cover of the 1913 book *The Poker Primer or, How to Play Poker.*

baccarat, where you gambled money on the turn of a card. Perhaps that was why it appealed to me at that time—for the risk and the machismo that goes with risk taking. It was the low point in my life, and all my usual principles were on hold. My first marriage had just unraveled, and I had recently quit university teaching to become a freelance writer. But with an ex-wife and child to support there was no time to write the books I'd planned. Instead, I was scraping together a living by reviewing books and writing articles for anyone who would hire me. So to gamble more than I could afford blindly, like a dare, seemed a dashing thing to do. It proved what was not otherwise apparent: that I was one of the boys, that I didn't care. It was also a misapprehension that cost me a good deal, both in money and self-esteem. I lost regularly and was fortunate that the people I played with in those days—a couple of scriptwriters and jobbing journalists, a crazy painter whose pictures didn't sell, a charming hustler who worked in the gray area between art movies and pornography—were as innocent and self-deluding as I was.

⊗ left: This cartoon warns of the dangers of gambling.

⊗ top: Cover of the 1868 book *How Gamblers Win, or the Secrets of Advantage Playing.*

⊗ opposite page: This embossed 1910 postcard by S. A. Solomon served as an invitation to a poker game.

Then one summer evening, a young American appeared in our game. He was a pale, sweating youth, grossly overweight, with a face like that of the oaf on the cover of *Mad* magazine—the same carrotty crew cut and freckles, the same small, close-set eyes. In comparison with our fast-talking, rather literary group, he seemed graceless and dull—a hick with no small talk and even less charm who didn't get our jokes and couldn't pick up on our allusions. But he cleaned us out effortlessly two weeks in a row, until the man who had brought him was told to withdraw the invitation.

He handled the cards like a professional, crisply and deftly, and all of us suspected he was cheating. We were flattering ourselves. Not even the most compulsive cardsharp would have bothered to fix the deck for a group of mugs like us. Anyone could have taken our money simply by playing the game as it should be played, by the book, while we gambled wildly, unable to believe that hands that had started well wouldn't necessarily finish that way or that we didn't have some secret, special claim on the chips we had recklessly contributed to the pot.

The money I lost to the fat American turned out to be a good investment. He shamed me by taking it so easily, calling every pathetic bluff, then turning over his hole cards and scooping in the pot casually, scarcely bothering to wait to see what I had—not even interested, as though my pretenses were below

the level of his attention. But humiliation is a great teacher, and two long nights of it taught me that I knew nothing about the game. If I was going to play poker I would have to study it. So I got hold of the classic introduction, Herbert O. Yardley's *The Education of a Poker Player*, and read it through twice—first incredulous that anyone could play so conservatively, then ashamed of my own naïveté. Then I went back to the game and tried to apply what I'd learned. For two years after that, I played by the book—that is, by Yardley, whom I solemnly reread cover-to-cover each Friday afternoon before I went to the game. And for two years, with a couple of minor hiccups, I didn't lose.

It was a good period. For the first time in my life I had money to spare in my pocket—one night I was so successful that I went out the next day and bought myself an E-type Jaguar—and I was earning it in a way I enjoyed. My bank manager smiled at me whenever we met, and the reviews I wrote weekly began to seem more pointless than ever. They became merely a way of filling in the days before I sat down at the poker table at 8:00 each Friday evening. For a few zany moments, I imagined I might be able to make a modest living without having to churn out an article or a book review every week. It was all nonsense, of course. I was nailed to literature for life, but because I found the sheer labor of writing so hard I was always casting around for other things I could do that would both give me pleasure and earn me a little money.

Poker, in those days, wasn't really one of them, despite my success in the mugs' game. It is a deep game, and you never stop learning. Forty years later, I'm still learning, although now, when I play in casinos instead of private houses, I've learned enough to know that I will never be as good as the professionals I sit down with. But I didn't know that back then, and I was spared further humiliation only because the call came to lecture for a term at an American university.

When I got back to London my regular Friday game had broken up, and there were no more easy pickings. I joined a sterner, more sophisticated group that met on Tuesday nights and began learning all over again. Everyone in the Tuesday game knew the odds and the intricacies and most had read Yardley. Although there were no more easy pickings, the pleasure of playing poker skillfully with other skillful players was keener, even when I lost, than the simple, ego-boosting satisfaction of taking money off mugs.

The Tuesday game was part of my life for twenty years, a permanent fixture around which the rest of my week was arranged, and it taught me two different styles of poker. Because it was a private game, we played a lot of what I now think of as Mickey Mouse variations—most of them hi-lo and with wild cards—designed to keep the players playing and give them an excuse to put money in the pot. The master of this style was John, who happens to be Australian, although he has lived most of his life in Europe and is as English as Eton and Oxford can make you—modest, hesitant, with beautiful, you-first manners and a barking laugh that make him seem alarmingly self-deprecating until he sits down at the poker table. Then his English mannerisms intensify almost to the point of eccentricity—he stirs his chips around like they're soup, fiddles irritably with his cards, sips his whisky, taps his foot, shifts about in his chair—and the innocence vanishes. And you begin to wonder if maybe all that English diffidence were itself a bluff, part of some arcane game he plays with his life, because John is a true games player, and rules exist for him only to be broken or twisted or turned on their heads. Most solid poker players wait for good cards, then try to make the maximum from them. John knows how to do that but prefers not to. Solid play bores him. The challenge, as he sees it, is to take bad cards and turn them into winners by outmaneuvering his opponents, raising

when he should fold, flat calling when he should raise, and bewildering everyone with illogic. He doesn't play his cards, he plays the other players, and that is a skill that only true mind-games players ever master. He and I have played together, on and off, for nearly thirty years and I still can't read him.

Mind-games playing is an art I've never properly mastered. It's all done with mirrors, by thinking back-to-front or laterally but never straight: "'Contrariwise,' continued Tweedledee, 'if it was so, it might be; and if it were so, it would be; but as it isn't, it ain't. That's logic.'" But it's only logic on Lewis Carroll's chess-board world through the looking-glass, and it only works in dealer's-choice games where wild cards rule, anything can happen, and the players are there to gamble, to beat the odds.

I myself enjoy risk but, as I said, I've never much cared for gambling. Rock climbing is a risky activity, and I love it as much as I love poker, but it seems riskier to the eye of the beholder than it is on the rock face. For the climber, the art is in controlling the risk, in being skillful enough and fit enough to minimize the element of chance. Poker has a similar relationship to gambling. Poker is about discipline and calculation; to bet on horses, dogs, and random lottery numbers, on a little ivory ball rattling around a roulette wheel or on raindrops sliding down a window pane is at worst an addiction, at best a romantic weakness. You have to believe in your luck, in your special relationship with fate, in the possibility that you are somehow chosen and blessed. Against all the evidence, you have to be an optimist.

Optimism has never been my strong suit, and, as I got older and played more regularly in Las Vegas, I lost interest in wild-card gambling variations of poker. But there was one Tuesday-night regular who shared my preference for the classical game. His name was Terry, and he was my introduction to what

⊗ opposite page: "Never bet on anything you can't shuffle." This photograph, circa 1900, depicts gun-toting men playing cards.

I innocently considered to be the real world—the cynical, hard-headed realm that lay all around literature but impinged on it only in American thrillers.

Terry looked like a heavy in a film noir, a massive, lowering man with a square head, a powerful belly, and a strong line in black humor, wisecracking and hardheaded, resolutely North American. He had run a floating craps game in Montreal when he was a teenager, and that had given him a taste for lowlifes that blossomed after he moved to London and made money in real estate. Age and illness have now forced him out of the action, but back then he played poker not just on Tuesdays, like the rest of us, but most nights of the week—seven-card stud at the Victoria Casino and the Sportsman, then strip-deck poker at the private clubs in Soho that opened when the legal casinos closed. Terry organized his life around poker. He was in his office every day, wheeling and dealing, from nine in the morning until four in the afternoon, when he went home and slept until ten. Then he showered, shaved, ate a light meal, and drove off to the casinos, arriving bright-eyed and implacably good-humored just when the amateurs were running out of steam. Although he wasn't a professional and didn't

⊗ A card-game scene from the 1951 20th Century Fox movie *A Streetcar Named Desire.*

need the money, he played with the pros and he played in their style. He also shared their carefree indifference to money. He used to say, "When I do business deals and play poker, I want to be a tiger. With friends it's different." He was a frightening man to play cards with but absurdly generous to people he liked.

The Tuesday game was my poker college, but Terry put me on the road to higher education, and Las Vegas was my graduate school. "Las Vegas is like a parasite that feeds on money," a local poker professional once told me. "It sits here in the middle of the desert and produces absolutely nothing, yet it supports half a million people." That was in 1981. Since then, the parasite has more than doubled in size and grown subtler in its methods of extracting money from visitors, but its spirit remains the same. Behind the illusion—the fantasy worlds of the casinos, the cascading lights, the remorseless cheerfulness—lies the profoundest disillusion. It is, quite simply, the most cynical place on earth.

But its cynicism is also its saving grace—a form of vitality so shameless that it is endearing. Years ago, for example, when George Burns was performing at Caesar's Palace, I called to book a table. A rasping voice at the other end said, "Whaddya want? The 10:00 show or the midnight show?"

"Which do you recommend?"

"The guy's eighty-eight years old. Take the 10:00 show."

Even the maitre d' was working out the odds. In Vegas, everybody has an angle, from the casino bosses to the saddest cocktail waitress. They weigh you up in gold and call it the golden rule: he who has the gold makes the rules.

(Among those who have the gold, that rule, too, creates problems. A Texas millionaire once took offense at the outlandish VIP treatment a casino was dishing out to the Australian tycoon and highest of high rollers, Kerry Packer: the bevies of beautiful girls and fawning assistants around Packer were larger than those around him. "What makes you so special?" he asked Packer. "I've got a hundred million dollars in the bank."

"That's very impressive," billionaire Packer replied solemnly. "I tell you what: I'll toss you for it.")

Las Vegas is a peculiarly American creation: a resort surrounded by a cordon sanitaire of desert and designed simply to take money from vacationers by cashing in on their dreams and never giving a sucker an even break. I didn't know that when I first went there, in 1980, with my second wife and kids. I simply thought I'd died and gone to poker heaven; there were games everywhere and of all sizes, twenty-four hours a day. I'd never played in a casino before. I thought it would be like the Tuesday game where everybody ran outrageous bluffs, showed off, and had fun. Instead, it was as dour and unrelenting as laboring in a salt mine. I played for three days and lost steadily. But I loved the energy of the place, its arrogance and brutal swagger, and I came away feeling that I had paid my dues and that justice had been done.

The following year, I went back and stayed for three weeks. I wanted to know if I had the discipline and hardheadedness to play poker in the same style as the professionals. Poker of the kind that is played in Vegas has nothing to do with the adrenaline rush. On the contrary, it is about patience and self-control, and for an impatient person like myself to play in that way wasn't easy, despite all the efforts I'd made back in London. I'd read the books and talked about what was needed. Now I wanted to put my money where my mouth was.

I had gone back to Vegas to write a long piece for the *New Yorker* about the World Series of Poker, a competition that is held each May at Binion's Horseshoe Casino to decide who will be world champion for the year. (The article finished up as *The Biggest Game in Town*, the only book I have ever enjoyed writing.) The World Series is now poker's equivalent of Wimbledon, and poker players flood in from all over the globe to play in it, but it had started, in 1970, as a casual get-together of the high-rolling Texan cronies of Benny Binion, the owner of the Horseshoe, and when I first went there eleven years later the Texans were still in the majority: cowboys in alligator boots, wildcatters wearing Stetsons and Dior ties, gnarled good old boys who farmed in West Texas and had eyes like ferrets. I felt like I had walked into a Sam Peckinpah movie. Almost none of them had even heard of the *New Yorker* and they reacted to my English accent warily, as if it were some shrewd play I was trying to put them on. But not the highest rollers of all—men like Jack Straus, Doyle Brunson, and Eric Drache, who regularly played for hundreds of thousands of dollars and could handle any company.

They read me as easily as they read their opponents at the poker table, saw that I was genuinely interested, and decided they liked me because I could listen and make them laugh. So they let me sit in as a spectator on their giant games where the kind of money that would have made me rich for life changed hands as casually as small change.

Since that initiation, I have been back at Binion's for the World Series every May. Or almost every May; the years when I couldn't rustle up enough money to go were always a harsh reminder of the sorry state I was in. In 1994, again courtesy of the *New Yorker*, I even competed in the World Championship itself—the $10,000 buy-in no-limit hold 'em event. I suspect I am the only published poet to have done so. But it's hard to take notes and concentrate on the game at the same time, so I didn't do well. That story comes later.

Poker, as it is played in casinos by professionals, is a ruthless game. That is what I like about it and why I owe it something that has nothing to do with playing cards. Quite simply, poker taught me qualities I lacked—patience and cool-headedness—that steadied me when I most needed them.

When I first began to play in the Friday mugs' game, I was in my late twenties and had the profound ignorance that often goes with excessive education. I had been through the most high-minded academic mill, read a vast number of books, and written a couple of my own, but in my personal life I was naive to a degree that still makes me blush. I had a marriage I couldn't handle, a childish desire to be loved by the whole world, and an equally childish conviction that everything would turn out right in the end. I lived my life as I played poker, recklessly and optimistically, with my cards open on the table and nothing in reserve. I also assumed that everybody else was doing the same.

I was wrong, of course, and it was about the time I began to realize this that I first read Yardley's book.

Read: "You should study your own weaknesses as well as those of your opponents. Keep a poker face. Keep silent. Don't gripe when you lose a hand or gloat over a winning one." Read, above all: "A card player should learn that once the money is in the pot it isn't his any longer. His judgment should not be influenced by this. He should instead say to himself, 'Do the odds favor my playing regardless of the money I have already contributed?'" What was true of money in a card game was equally true of the feelings I had invested in my disastrous personal affairs: "Do the odds favor my playing regardless of what I had already contributed?" I knew the answer. The only puzzle was why I should have discovered it not in Shakespeare or Donne or Eliot or Lawrence or any of my other literary heroes, but in a how-to book about cards written by an American cryptographer. It was more than absurd; it was humiliating, an insult to all the effort I had made. But it was the beginning of my own education in the ways of the world beyond literature, and I sometimes wonder if that was what Yardley, too, was implying when he called his book *The Education of a Poker Player*. In the end, what he is describing is not so much a game of cards as a style of life.

⊗ opposite page: Benny Binion is shown in front of his Horseshoe Casino in Las Vegas. His motto was "Trust everyone but always shuffle the cards."

⊗ above: Contestants in the first World Series of Poker at Binion's Horseshoe Casino in Las Vegas, 1970.

LARGEST WEEKLY CIRCULATION IN AMERICA

TIP TOP WEEKLY

AN
IDEAL PUBLICATION
FOR THE AMERICAN YOUTH

Issued Weekly. By Subscription $2.50 per year. Entered as Second Class Matter at New York Post Office by STREET & SMITH, 238 William St., N. Y.

No. 450.   Price, Five Cents.

DICK MERRIWELL IN LONDON
OR EXPOSING THE RASCALS

BY
BURT L. STANDISH

Budthorne suddenly bent over the table and grasped one of Bunol's wrists. A moment later he
tore from the fellow's sleeve the hold-out containing five cards.

SHAKESPEARE · ON · POKER

"Out, damned spot
Out, I say."

Macbeth
act V.-scene I.

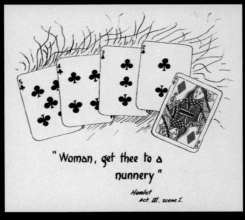

"Woman, get thee to a
nunnery"

Hamlet
Act. III. scene I.

"The Queen being absent, 'tis a
needful fitness that we adjourn
this court."

King Henry VIII.
act II - scene IV.

⊗ opposite page: Cover of an issue of *Tip Top Weekly*,
a popular weekly magazine for boys.

⊗ above: Title page and illustrations from the 1906 book
Shakespeare on Poker, in which Shakespearean quotes
are given dubious interpretation.

AMERICAN *the* GAME

You talk of your cricket and your baseball, your golf and tennis and football. You can have them. They're all very well—for boys. Is it a reasonable thing, I ask you, for a grown man to run about and hit a ball?

Poker's the only game fit for a grown man. Then, your hand is against every man's, and every man's hand is against yours. Teamwork? Who ever made a fortune by teamwork? There's only one way to make a fortune, and that's to down the fellow who's up against you.

Somerset Maugham, "Cosmopolitans"

⊗ This 1909 postcard, captioned "A Sunday School Class in the West," depicts an eight-handed poker game with a guard posted at the door. The photograph, by Charles E. Morris of Chinook, Montana, is color-tinted.

I SUSPECT THAT ALL US NOVICES in the feckless Friday night sessions where I learned to play were drawn to poker because we were in love with America, and poker is the most American of games. It is, in fact, America's national game, though the casual visitor would never guess it from television or the sports pages or the way the fans talk during the run up to the World Series or the Super Bowl, when nothing seems more important to the average American than baseball or football.

However, baseball and football are spectator sports, and, airtime and column inches notwithstanding, not many people go on playing them once they have left school and lost their physical edge. Poker, in comparison, is a game for life and a great equalizer—what the young gain from stamina the old make up for with experience—and it is played by at least sixty million Americans. Sixty million may even be a conservative estimate. John Scarne, one of the great modern authorities on gambling, reckoned that 95 percent of the people he knew had played poker at some time or another. Scarne, of course, moved in high-rolling circles, so his figures may be skewed, but whatever the exact numbers, one thing is clear: poker is more than the national game; it is part of the American way of life—the treasured part that allows Americans to indulge in their passion for toughness without the tedious business of staying trim and fit.

The hardest poker games in the world are played in Las Vegas, and the people who do well in them are mental athletes as tough as the toughest quarterback. They just don't look the part. That haggard young man behind a mountain of chips, his face shrouded by dark glasses and the pulled-down brim of his cap, can calculate in his head, to two decimal places, the odds on any proposition. The jovial Texan says, "Howdy, pardner" when you sit down, then frightens the life out of you with a brutal check-raise. The disdainful Asian with a duck's-ass haircut curling over the collar of his leather jacket and a pretty Hispanic girlfriend sitting patiently at his elbow comes out betting like Genghis Khan whenever he senses weakness. All of them are world-class players, but no one would ever guess it from their appearance.

In his *Book of Tells*, Mike Caro explains, with great subtlety, how to distinguish a bluff from the real

⊗ opposite page: Bobby Baldwin, World Champion of 1978.

European casinos, still hankering for a past when gambling was glamorous, have a fussy dress code: no jeans, no T-shirts, no sneakers. In America anything goes: tattered sweatshirts or Italian printed silks, Stetsons, Andy Capp flat hats, baseball caps with arcane insignia, heavy bracelets and rings, expensive watches, and lucky charms. (I once sat down with a player who had an ominous golden revolver nestling in his chest hair. He lost consistently.) At the poker table, clothes tell you nothing about the person except perhaps that he thinks one of the garments he is wearing will bring him luck.

None of this fashion show means a thing; nobody cares; nobody even notices. And this is another of the many reasons why poker is America's national game: it is a truly democratic activity. Race, color, creed, what you look like, where you come from, and what you do for a living are of no interest at all. A little green man from a distant galaxy could sit down and play without anyone blinking, provided he had the necessary amount of chips in front of him and anted up on time.

Few of the millions of Americans who play poker have mastered the intricacies of the game—the percentages, the moves, the immutable odds—that would enable them to survive in the killing fields of Las Vegas, but most have the hang of it and know the lingo. And they learn it young, starting with family games for nickels and dimes at the kitchen table with an older brother and sister and maybe a widowed aunt; then playing in college for however much the student grant will bear; then on to bigger games at golf clubs and in private houses. Poker is generally reckoned to be America's second most popular after-dark activity. And even there it has the edge. "Sex is good," they say, "but poker lasts longer."

Poker is to Americans what chess is to the Russians, cricket to the English and motor-racing to the

thing by analyzing your opponent's body language. Whether he leans forward or back in his seat may tell you something about his cards, but what he is wearing and how he looks physically mean nothing at all. Which is just as well, since poker players generally are an unprepossessing bunch. They slouch in their chairs around the table, their eyes are muddy, their paunches sag, their skin is soggy and unaired. They sleep irregularly at the wrong hours and eat irregularly the wrong food. They smoke too much and rarely exercise. But many of them were athletes in their youth, and they turned to poker because their desire to compete and win lingered on long after their legs gave out. In memory of their vanished prowess, they often wear sloppy track suits when they play.

⊗ "Amarillo Slim" Preston, World Champion of 1972.

Italians. The game is part of the culture, and its terms are embedded in the language. Perhaps that widowed aunt has a past that mom and pop prefer not to mention because she seems a different, more eagle-eyed person with a deck of cards in her hand. She shuffles them stylishly and snaps them out like a riverboat gambler, with a running commentary between each card: "Ace to the deuce, cowboy to the lady, trey to the trey. Pair of treys bets." For the kid with his pile of small change it sounds like magic, an incantation that will initiate him into the adult world.

Yet that alluring hocus-pocus is merely the stylized end of a vocabulary he will use unthinkingly for the rest of his life. Philologists say that language is full of dead metaphors. The word "attend," for instance, comes from the Latin words "ad," "to" or "towards," and "tendere," which means "to stretch"; when I attend to you I stretch my ears toward you. Ralph Waldo Emerson, using a dead metaphor himself, called language "fossilized poetry." American vernacular is full of fossilized poker terms: "bluff," "showdown," "something up your sleeve," "above board" (that is, with your cards on the table, not under it), and "passing the buck" (the "buck" is a marker that goes around the table to indicate who is dealing; these days it is usually an oval disk marked "dealer," but in frontier times it was a clasp knife with a buckhorn handle). As the kid grows up he will learn that "four flushers" aren't to be trusted and that if he has to "play against a stacked deck" and "the odds are against him" his "ace in the hole" will be to "play his cards close to his chest," to "up the ante," "stand pat," and rely on adult virtues like fortitude—"keeping a poker face"—and honesty—"putting his cards on the table." He will learn, in fact, that there is a poker expression for almost everything: "Read 'em and weep" for triumph, "Shut up and deal" for impatience, and, for grave moments of

⊗ top two images: These playful poker bucks date from the early 20th century.

⊗ bottom two images: Mid-19th-century American ivory poker bucks, the markers that indicate who is dealing the hand.

⊗ above: "Poker is the art of civilized bushwhacking," Jon Bradshaw. This painting was used in the 1895 book *It's All in the Draw*, by C. E. H. Brelsford and C. W. Dimick.

⊗ right: *California Gold Rush*, an 1879 albumen print of gold miners playing cards.

⊗ below: Duck hunters play poker in this photo from around the 1940s.

decision, "The chips are down." With luck, he will have made some "blue-chip investments" (blue usually being the color of the most expensive chip in the game) before he himself "cashes in his chips" or "taps out." American vernacular is so saturated with poker terms that it seems almost impossible to live life without playing the game.

In *Poker Faces*, David Hayano, a poker-playing sociologist, remarked, "Poker is not a game in which the meek inherit the earth." Nor did they inherit America. It took an altogether freer and more adventurous spirit to open up the vast, indifferent landscape, settle it, cultivate it, and sustain, against the odds, an orderly way of life. "Those who live in the midst of democratic fluctuations have always before their eyes the image of chance," wrote Alexis de Tocqueville in his great work, *Democracy in America*; "and they end by liking all undertakings in which chance plays a part." De Tocqueville was writing from the point of view of a European, habituated to a hierarchical society and fascinated by the brave new world where they ordered these things differently. Life itself was a gamble in a wide-open democracy, where class distinctions were fluid, everyone was on the move, and the possibility of going from log cabin to White House wasn't a foolish dream. In the melting pot of the frontier nothing, not even the law, was fixed or stable, and self-reliance was the secret of survival— self-reliance and the ability to cash in on a winning streak and "play your rush." Gambling and pioneering went together; both thrived on great expectations, risk-taking, opportunism, and a willingness to fold a losing hand and move on. All these qualities came together in poker: you could beat the odds with skill, self-control, and hardheaded calculation. It was the perfect frontier game.

Perhaps this is why it took so long to catch on in straight-laced nineteenth-century England, although it was introduced by no less lofty a figure than General Robert Schenck, the American ambassador to the court of St. James. One weekend during the summer of 1872, while Schenck was staying at the Somerset country house of a certain "Lady W," the conversation turned to cards. What followed is recorded by W. J. Florence in his *Handbook on Poker* (1891):

During this talk he described to her the beauties of poker in such a way that she became intensely interested, and begged him to write her out a set of rules and directions for playing the great American game. This Mr. Schenck very kindly did. The duchess learned to play poker, and as it wove its fascinating toils about her she wanted her friends to learn also. For convenience she had Mr. Schenck's letter printed in a neat pamphlet and distributed among her friends of the court circles.

When a copy of the pamphlet was circulated back in America it was much criticized, not least because Schenck's rules are vague, not particularly accurate, and at times downright misleading. For instance, position at the poker table is supremely important; the dealer, who is last to bet or check or raise, always has an edge on the other players. Yet Schenck's opening words are, "The deal is of no special value, and anybody may begin. The dealer, beginning with the person on his left, throws around five cards to each player." His hazy rules and cavalier attitude to detail, however, are not the reasons why the English were reluctant to take up poker. It was, instead, a question of national temperament. The nature of the game and the pleasures it offered— feinting, counterpunching, outsmarting your neighbor, bluffing him out of his winning hands, and never giving a sucker an even break—went against British ideals of probity and fair play. Poker didn't take off in England until after World War II and the collapse of the British empire. In a trivial way, it was the Old Country's introduction to the cynical, tough-minded modern world.

But there was something about the combination of cards and money, cut-throat psychology and beady-eyed skill that suited the American frontier spirit just fine. As Walter Matthau once said, "The game exemplifies the worst aspects of capitalism that have made our country so great." Poker, he meant, is a form of social Darwinism in which only the socially and economically fittest survive. It depends on making your own luck rather than on being lucky.

Luck helps, of course, and you must know how to use it when it comes. "Opportunity may knock," David Mamet once wrote, "but it seldom nags." Sometimes the cards run unreasonably in your favor, you fill every hand you draw to, and the laws of probability seem temporarily on hold. When that happens you must play your rush and be grateful. Sometimes they run against you no matter how well you play. Then all you can do is bow your head, sit tight, and wait for the storm to blow itself out. Either way, poker is about winning and the disciplines necessary for this: calculation, insight, deception, ruthlessness, and, above all, the virtue Texans call "a leather ass"— known elsewhere as patience.

"The worst aspects of capitalism which have made our country so great" are illustrated most vividly in *The Education of a Poker Player*, first published in 1957 and still going strong. Yardley was blessed with a talent for mathematics and a photographic memory, and he used his gifts to the full— as a cryptographer and a government spy as well as a successful poker player. He began playing in 1905, when he was sixteen, and served his poker apprenticeship in the back room of Monty's saloon in Worthington, Indiana, a little frontier town where poker,

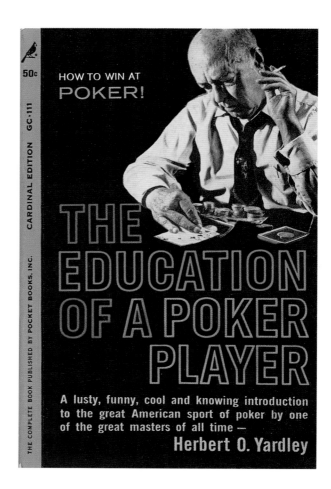

⊗ Cover from Herbert O. Yardley's 1957 book *The Education of a Poker Player.*

booze, and whoring were the only entertainment on offer to red-blooded men:

I saw the big Swede, Bones Alverson, a poor weather-beaten corn farmer, bet the last of his farm against a tent show, only to die three minutes later, his cards clutched in his hands—a winner.

I saw Jake Moses, a travelling shoe salesman, lose ten trunks of shoes. I saw a bank teller trapped with marked money he had stolen from the bank; a postmaster go to jail for shortages at the post office.

Horses, cattle, hogs, wagons, buggies, farming implements, grain, sawmills—all sold to play poker. New owners showed up at the sawmills, feed and grocery stores.

This, of course, led to frequent fights—some tragic. My own uncle, a giant of a man with a Jesse James beard, was cut down by a consumptive half his size. Uncle Bill walked a block, sat down on the corner drugstore steps, and bled to death.

Yardley's stories are dramatic, simple, and loving, like the folktales collected by the Brothers Grimm. And in a way, that is what they are: the mythology of America on the move, the winners winning, the losers going under, social Darwinism in action.

Each story illustrates a particular form of the game that was most popular at the time—draw, stud, hi-lo, and some of their variations—and includes Yardley's peculiarly stringent rules for winning. These rules themselves illustrate another, sterner aspect of the cynical reality behind the American dream. The classical game Yardley teaches is not only conservative, it is also deeply pessimistic. "I do not believe in luck," he writes, "only in the immutable law of averages." In Yardley's style of poker there is no room for play in any of the frivolous senses of the word. Frivolity, quite simply, is too expensive. What his advice amounts to is, Assume the worst, believe no one, and make your move only when you are certain either that your hand is unbeatable or that the odds are strongly in your favor.

This is the only way to play against weak players, and Yardley seems to have been blessed with a disproportionate number of them during his years at the poker table. The simple rule is, Never try to bluff a simpleton, because he won't understand what you're doing. He's not asking himself, "What can you have?" Instead, he's thinking, "Wow! Look what I've got!" So he calls on his puny pair of deuces. With sophisticated players, Yardley's rules are less effective; they will recognize a "rock" when they see him and adjust their game accordingly, turning his tight play to their advantage. That, however, was not Yardley's business. He was a purist writing for embryo purists, concerned only with the rules and values of classical poker. He was also setting out an iron-clad system for survival in the hostile environment of the American frontier.

CHAPTER 2

Origins: **FROM GAMBLING** *to* **SCIENCE**

Opposite the bankholder stood some of the smart speculators and specialists in gambling who, like old criminals, were no longer afraid of the galley. They came to play three stakes and disappeared immediately after having won their livelihood.

Honoré de Balzac, *La peau de chagrin*

⊗ This card is from the Persian game As-Nas, from which some
believe poker to have originated.

POKER WAS ASSIMILATED INTO AMERICAN CULTURE SO FAST

and so thoroughly that some historians maintain that the game is at least as old as Columbus's discovery of America and that its origins are almost as old as Western civilization itself. According to this theory, poker was derived from a Persian game called As-Nas and was brought into the country by Columbus's sailors. As-Nas, in its turn, was said to be an ancient game, dating back many hundreds of years, like chess.

Like the stories that surround most myths, this one is a mixture of truth and fiction. The true part is that As-Nas and Old Poker, as it was first played in New Orleans, were virtually the same game—a game played by four players with a twenty-card deck in which the ace was the key card. In an As-Nas deck, there were four aces, kings, ladies, soldiers, and dancing girls; in the European deck, the ladies were elevated to queens and the scandalous dancing girl became plain Jane ten. In both games, each player was dealt five cards, then each bet on them, without a draw, according to their combinations: pairs, trips, full houses (so called because they are the only combination in which all five cards are used), and four of a kind. (Straights and flushes didn't arrive until after 1837, when the game was adapted to a full 52-card deck.) The ace was the all-powerful card because there were only two hands in a twenty-card deck that could not be beaten: four aces and four kings with an ace. (The ace with the kings, of course, meant that no one else could be holding four aces.)

Those are the facts, but the antiquity of the game is fiction. There is no evidence that Columbus's sailors played poker or that As-Nas itself was played earlier than the seventeenth century, the date of its oldest surviving cards. It may not even have been a Persian game. Instead, it seems most likely that it was invented by the French diplomats, administrators, and merchants who were serving their country in Persia (Iran) around the beginning of the nineteenth century and adapted their own game of *poque* or *bouillotte* to the local As-Nas deck, then taught it to their Persian hosts.

There are two reasons for believing in this French connection, and the vital clue in both is the word "ace." First, there was no ace in the original As-Nas decks. Each deck was a work of art, elaborate, hand

⊗ These Old Florentine designs for playing cards are from a series of eight.

painted and unique; no two of them were alike, and their beauty was an indication of their owners' social status and wealth. But the most powerful card they contained, ranking higher than the king, was the lion or the sun. "As," in fact, is not even a relevant Farsi (Persian) word, as David Partlett pointed out in *A History of Card Games* (Oxford, 1990, p. 112), "but it does happen to be the French for 'Ace.'" The second clue is the key role the ace played in As-Nas and poker. "As" may not be a relevant Farsi word, but "As-Naz"—"Naz" spelled with a "z" instead of an "s"—means "my beloved ace," and that is a cry that has been echoed by countless poker players for as long as the game has been played.

In other words, As-Nas was merely the five-card Persian version of a family of related European three-card games with similar rules and similar ways of ranking the hands—pairs, three of a kind, and three of the same suit, a "flux" or "flush." All of them were gambling games in which how and when you bet played an important part. Hence the concept of bluff. At a crucial, early point in the development of the games, some smart guy must have realized that a large raise could drive out a hand that was stronger than his, but not invincible. As Shelley almost said, "If betting comes, can bluff be far behind?" "Bluff," in the early years, was an alternative name for poker. In England, the three-card variant, which is still widely played, is called "brag"; bragging or boasting is closely related to the idea of bluffing. Brag itself was developed from the Spanish and Italian primero, which may have been the game Columbus's sailors brought with them across the Atlantic. In Germany, the game was called pochspiel; *pochen* means "to knock" and when a player bet, say, ten units, he would rap the table and say, "*Ich poche zehn*." The French adopted that phrase into their own variation, bouillotte—the bettor would announce, "*Je poque de dix*"—and eventually their game became known as poque. Since all the experts agree that American poker originated in the early years of the nineteenth century in what, until the Louisiana Purchase of 1803, had been the French colonial city of New Orleans, its most likely antecedent has to be poque. The French pronounce poque as a word with two syllables. To an English speaker with a lazy Southern drawl, that would have sounded like "pok-ah" and been transcribed as "poker."

From the casinos of New Orleans the game spread north up the Mississippi, following the easy money on the steamboats to St. Louis, then west with the gold rush to California. The first decades of the nineteenth century were a period of great wealth in the South. The railroad had linked the cotton fields to the great river, and the thriving towns along its banks—Vicksburg, Natchez, Memphis—were crowded with professional gamblers on the lookout for rich suckers. For them, Old Poker played, As-Nas style, with a twenty-card deck, was even more profitable than a straightforward con game like three-card monte. Even the dumbest mark was unlikely to be swindled often by three-card monte, but in poker the trickery was less obvious. The cards were shuffled and cut between each deal, so it seemed like a legitimate game.

It was nothing of the kind. Old Poker, played with five cards dealt to each player, then bet and shown down without a draw to upset the distribution of the cards, was an ideal game for cardsharps, and the Mississippi steamboats were the ideal setup. They were kitted out as floating palaces and crowded with plantation owners flush with money and determined to have themselves some fun, no matter how much it cost them. It was the business of the ships' officers to make sure they got whatever they wanted, and since most

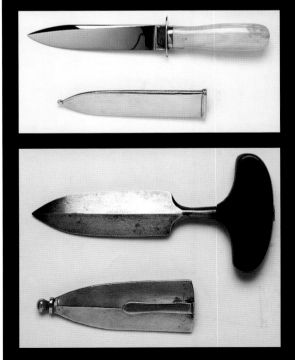

⊗ top: This late-19th-century Will and Finck sleeve card-holdout, used for cheating at poker, required the cheater to wear an extra-wide cuff. Will and Finck specialized in making cheating devices for gamblers.

⊗ right, top: This mid-19th-century American walrus-ivory-handled bowie knife, by Michael Price, was typical of the defense weapons carried by professional gamblers. Although they were usually hidden, gamblers liked them to be stylish.

⊗ right, bottom: The mid-19th-century American-made gambler's-style push dagger was commonly used by Mississippi riverboat gamblers. The vogue of the inconspicuous arms came west with gamblers who were migrating from New Orleans.

⊗ above: This 1890 sterling silver matchsafe is in the American West gambler style. Matchsafes embossed with gambling images often served to let others in a salon know the carrier was interested in playing cards. It also often ended up in the pot when the owner ran out of chips.

of them wanted to gamble for high stakes, the officers often worked in cahoots with the cardsharps. Poker games were so much a part of the attraction of the riverboats that the various card-making companies used a common trade name: "Steamboat Playing Cards."

No wonder, then, that the first published description of the newfangled game of poker involved cheating and was located on a Mississippi steamer. It appeared in *Thirty Years Passed among the Players in England and America*, published in New York in 1844 and written by an Englishman named Joe Cowell. He himself was not a card-player, but he has earned himself a place in the history of poker as the first kibitzer. The game he described took place in December 1829, on board the steamboat *Helen M'Gregor*. Cowell was a sailor turned itinerant actor—the players in his title performed on the stage, not at the card table—and, being an actor, he wanted to milk as much drama as he could from his long boat ride from Louisville to New Orleans. Nobody, he realized, wants to read about games they don't know, but everyone is interested in bad behavior, especially when it involves sly gentlemen in tinted spectacles, with diamond stickpins in their cravats and heavy gold watch chains roped across their vests. He had hit upon what proved to be an

⊗ top left: David A. Curtis's 1906 *Stand Pat* is a collection of 20 short stories about poker games on riverboats and in towns along the Mississippi.

⊗ above: The "Steamboat" deck was the least expensive version of playing cards around the turn of the century, and each manufacturer had its own version. These examples are from 1890 to 1900.

irresistible formula. Thereafter, nineteenth-century pulp fiction is full of crooked poker games in which virtue inevitably triumphs and the cardsharp comes to a sticky end:

It was a foggy, wretched night. Our bell was kept tolling to warn other boats to our whereabouts or to entreat direction to a landing by a fire on the shore. Suddenly a most tremendous concussion, as if all-powerful Nature had shut his hand upon us, and crushed us all to atoms, upset our cards and calculations, and a general rush was made, over chairs and tables toward the doors. The cabin was entirely cleared, or, rather, all the passengers were huddled together at the entrances, with the exception of one of the poker players: a gentleman in green spectacles, a gold guard-chain, long and thick enough to moor a dog, and a brilliant diamond breast-pin; he was, apparently, quietly shuffling and cutting the poker pack for his own amusement. In less time than I am telling it, the swarm came laughing back, in which snags, bolts blown out, and boilers burst, were most conspicuous. But all the harm the fracas caused was fright; the boat, in rounding to a wood-pile, had run on to the point of an island, and was high and dry among a never-ending supply of fuel to feed this peculiar navigation, which alone can combat the unceasing, serpentine, tempestuous current of the I-will-have-my-own-way, glorious Mississippi.

The hubbub formed a good excuse to end our game which my stupidity had made desirable long before, and I took a chair beside the poker players, who, urged by the gentleman with the diamond pin, again resumed their seats. It was his turn to deal, and when he ended, he did not lift his cards, but sat watching quietly the countenances of the others. The man on his left had bet ten dollars; a young lawyer, son to the then Mayor of Pittsburgh, who little dreamed of what his boy was about, who had hardly recovered from his shock, bet ten more; at that time, fortunately for him, he was unconscious of the real value of his hand, and consequently did not betray by his manner, as greenhorns mostly do, his certainty of winning. My chicken friend bet that ten dollars and five hundred dollars better!

"I must see that," said Green Spectacles, who now took up his hand with "I am sure to win," trembling at his fingers' ends; for you couldn't see his eyes through his glasses; he paused a moment in disappointed astonishment, and sighed, "I pass," and threw his cards upon the table. The left-hand man bet "that five hundred dollars and one thousand dollars better!"

The young lawyer, who had had time to calculate the power of his hand—four kings with an ace—it could not be beat! but still he hesitated at the impossibility, as if he thought it could—looked at the money staked and then at his hand again, and, lingeringly, put his wallet on the table and called. The left-hand man had four queens, with an ace: and Washington, the four jacks and an ace.

"Did you ever see the like on't?" said he, good-humouredly, as he pushed the money towards the lawyer, who, very agreeably astonished, pocketed his two thousand and twenty-three dollars clear!

The truth was, the cards had been *put up*, or *stocked*, as it is called, by the guard-chain-man while the party were off their guard, or, rather, on the guard of the boat in the fog, inquiring if the boiler had burst; but the excitement of the time had caused him to make a slight mistake in the distribution of the hand; and young "Six-and-eight-pence" got the one he had intended for himself. He was one of many who followed card playing for a living but not properly coming under the denomination of

gentleman-sportsman, who alone depends on his superior skill. But in that pursuit, as in all others, even among the players, some black-sheep and black-legs will creep in, as in the present instance.

Joe Cowell's story confirmed the general belief that poker, in its original form, had a bad name. "A cheating game" is how a reformed gambler named Jonathan H. Green describes it in his book *The Exposure of the Arts and Miseries of Gambling* (New York, 1843). And even when the players were honest, Old Poker, played with a twenty-card deck by four players and without a change, was as much a gambling game as roulette.

All that began to change when poker was adapted to the full deck. Fifty-two cards meant that more than four people could play. It also meant that after the deal, even with six or seven players, there were still cards left in the deck to draw. This was a great encouragement to optimists, especially when the introduction of straights and flushes gave them something to be optimistic about. Players who wanted to stay in the action despite the cards they had been dealt could stick their money in the pot and hope to improve with the draw.

Optimism, in fact, was so endemic and poker so popular that, in 1870, a serious player from Toledo, Ohio, tried to sober up the game by introducing "jackpots" to draw poker: no one could open the betting unless he held two jacks or better. The idea was to impose discipline on the game by protecting cautious players who held fair-to-middling cards from being scared out by wild men and bullies who bet and raised with nothing, merely for the hell of it. The introduction of the fifty-two-card deck and then of jackpots were the first steps in the process that transformed poker from a gambling game into a science.

The traditionalists had no problem with playing with a full deck, but they didn't take easily to jackpots. In 1880, John Blackridge, author of *The Complete Poker Player*, missed the point of jackpots entirely when he called them "equivalent to a lottery except that all players must buy tickets." This was a paradoxical use of the word "lottery" since the whole purpose of the rule was to ensure that at least one player would have a passable hand before he threw money into the pot. Even so, the resentment about jackpots lingered on. A quarter of a century later, another traditionalist, R. F. Foster, was still complaining in his book *Practical Poker* (1904): "The jack-pot, with its accompanying small-limit game, has completely killed bluffing—that pride and joy of the old-timer. Modern poker has gradually become more of a lottery than anything else." Foster at least understood the purpose of the innovation and grudgingly accepted its inevitability. "The two great steps in the history and progress of Poker," he concluded, "have undoubtedly been the introduction of the draw to

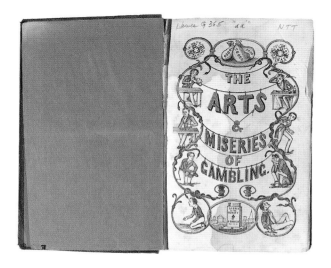

⊗ left: Jonathan Harrington Green's *The Exposure of the Arts and Miseries of Gambling,* published in 1843, is the second book ever to mention poker. This is the opening page of the second edition.

⊗ opposite page left: Two mid-19th-century ivory poker bucks.

⊗ opposite page right: Covers of two issues of *Poker Chips,* a monthly magazine devoted to stories of the great American game.

improve the hand, and the invention of the jack-pot as a cure for cautiousness. It has come to stay." Players in the Western and Eastern states agreed with him, although high-rolling Southern gentlemen considered jackpots a wimpish variation, below their dignity, and they took years to adapt to it.

Part of the genius of poker is its endless capacity for development. Jackpots are merely one of literally hundreds of variations: Cincinnati, Chicago, anaconda, Levy's game, the don's game, fiery cross, screw your neighbor, spit in the ocean, elevator, and so on. Every social game, like every ambitious restaurant, has its own speciality of the house, most of them involving wild cards. Once upon a time, in the course of a particularly unhappy evening, some disgruntled player must have said, "All I'm getting is worthless cards—deuces, treys, fours. Let's play a game where the low cards beat the big ones." And that's how lowball, razz, misère, and hi-lo were born.

Essentially, all these games, even the craziest, are variations on two basic themes: closed or draw poker, in which all the cards are dealt facedown, and stud, in which four of the player's five or seven cards are dealt faceup. Stud was a cowboy game, named after the stud horse, and first played in the middle of the nineteenth century around Ohio, Indiana, and Illinois. It spread west with the pioneers and introduced a whole new dimension of skill into the game.

To play either form well you need to know the odds and percentages, the chances of hitting your cards, and the correct price to pay for them. You also need to read (you hope) your opponents' cards. In closed poker, where none of the cards are exposed, there are only two ways of doing that. The first is deduction: When and how much did they bet? How many cards did they draw? The second is observation: their body language, the expression in their eyes, their nervous tics. Jennings Perry put it best in a short

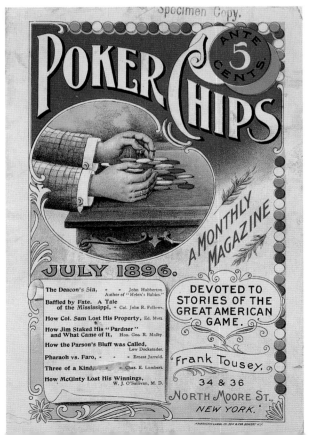

story called "Poker Face": "You play it with your hands and your face—but mostly with your face." In stud the same principles apply, but the exposed cards give you extra information, which helps you calculate which cards the other players have, or don't have, in the hole.

A long time ago, for example, I was playing seven-card stud in an illegal, after-hours club near London's Piccadilly Circus. It was a seedy joint, with a steel door and a peephole, and it stank of sour frying oil. The proprietor was a menacing bull of a man, an ex-cop who had been forcibly retired from the service for tampering, in every sense, with a teenage girl witness. He had gotten to know most of the players during his time with the Metropolitan police. They were small-time crooks—burglars, pimps, con men—people who worked nights, wanted to play cards after the legal casinos closed, and preferred cash to chips; there were wads of soiled banknotes on the table, plenty more in their pockets, and no questions asked about where they got it from. There were also a few professional players in the game, as there always are when there is easy money around. One of them was a long-haired hippie, wearing a caftan and apparently high on some controlled substance; he had so many twitches and tics that none of them seemed significant. He was also afflicted with a stutter so crippling that he could scarcely string two words together. At one point during the long night, he called a large bet by someone show-ing what seemed, to my innocent eye, a certain straight. When the hippie turned over his two small pairs and raked in the pot, the outraged bluffer shouted, "How could you possibly call me?" The hippie opened his bleary eyes and said, "You c-c-c-couldn't huff-huff-huff had a s-s-s-s-straight." Then he reeled off every card that had fallen during the deal. And he didn't stutter once. Apart from me, everybody at the table knew him, so his stutter was obviously not a bluff.

He was simply a man with a photographic memory, and whenever it clicked in his stutter vanished. He was also a true professional: he watched, he waited, he counted the cards, worked out the odds, and never contributed to a pot unless he thought he had the best of it; but when he did so he was fearless.

Seven-card stud is still widely played, but the five-card variation more or less vanished around 1980. At that time the great master of five-card stud was Bill Boyd, a courtly gentleman from Arkansas who was usually referred to, even by his friends, as Mr. Boyd. Mr. Boyd, who ran the poker room at the Golden Nugget in Las Vegas for thirty-six years, until he retired in 1982, was generally recognized to be the finest five-card stud player in America. His picture is up in Binion's Poker Hall of Fame, and even "Amarillo Slim" Preston, a man not famous for his modesty, once said, "I'd rather catch frost on my winter peaches than play stud with Bill Boyd." Mr. Boyd's skill in reading his opponents' cards and mak-ing unconventional moves was uncanny. David Spanier described one of his greatest coups in *The Little Book of Poker*:

CzN

JUNE 25¢

Easy Money
How it's Made - How it's Lost

In This Issue:

PICKING DERBY WINNERS
HAUPTMANN - a Jersey Industry

⊗ opposite page: Clark Gable in a scene from MGM's 1939 film *Gone with the Wind.* Rhett Butler, the Southern gentleman, is playing poker with his Yankee captors in Atlanta during the Civil War.

⊗ this page: Cover of the June 1936 issue of the magazine *Easy Money.*

[Boyd] had been beaten out of $50,000 by a boastful player who made a lucky outdraw, and who then left the big game to brag about his prowess at a lower level. One night Bill followed him down and the following hand developed.

Player: (x) Q-4-4-10

Bill: (x) 9-3-3-Q

At the opening, the queen bet $70 and Bill raised $200 on his 9. The other players passed. On the third card Mr. Show-off was quite sure he had best hand, whether Bill had paired his 9s or had an ace in the hole, and bet $500. Bill made it $1,000. His opponent merely called. (Of course he should have raised the roof, to win the pot then and there.)

On the fourth card Show-off, feeling confident, bet $2,000. Bill called and raised $6,000. Naturally the man had to see. And on the last card Bill bet the pot, $18,600. The man called for what he had left, $16,100.

You guessed it—Bill had a 3 in the hole. His opponent who had queens wired simply could not believe Bill would have started out on a (3) 9. The pot was worth $50,800. Bill tipped the dealer $800 and said: "That makes me evens."

Mr. Boyd won the five-card stud title at the World Series of Poker at Binion's Horseshoe every year it was played, so regularly and inevitably that in the end no one else bothered to enter the event and it was dropped from the schedule. By the time he died, in 1997, at the age of ninety-one, his mastery was so absolute that he had eliminated the opposition and the game effectively died out.

⊗ above: Bill Boyd (right), for decades the American master of five-card stud, with Irish gambler Terry Rogers.

⊗ opposite page: This player's license plate promotes his favorite game: hold 'em, a variation of seven-card stud.

Five-card stud is still occasionally played in conservative private games but not in public card rooms. The game that has replaced it is Texas hold 'em and its four-card variant, Omaha. Hold 'em is a variation of seven-card stud in which five of the seven cards are communal. Each player is dealt two cards facedown, "in the hole." The two players to the left of the dealer are forced to bet "blind"—before they see their cards. The other players cannot check; they either call the blind bet or raise it or fold. Then three communal cards, called the "flop," are dealt faceup in the center of the table, and there is another round of betting, although this time the players may check. Then two more communal cards—known as "Fourth Street" or "the turn," and "Fifth Street" or "the river"—are dealt faceup, one at a time, with a round of betting or checking after each. The five cards in the center are common to all the players, who use them in combination with their hole cards to make the strongest possible hands.

Omaha is played the same way, except that each player is dealt four cards facedown, instead of two, and each must use two of them. Having to use two of your four hole cards makes Omaha a very different game from hold 'em and creates very different situations. In hold 'em a pair of aces in the hole is the strongest possible starting hand. In Omaha a pair of aces and a pair of kings double suited (Ah-As-Kh-Ks) is equally strong, but four running cards, such as K-Q-J-10 or 9-8-7-6, are almost as powerful, because once the flop is dealt anything can happen. Say, for example, that you have raised with your double-suited aces and kings, a player calls you with Jd-10d-7c-6c, and the flop is 9h-8s-2c. You may be ahead at the moment, but if you bet, your opponent is going to raise you, sure as sunrise, because there are twenty-four cards in the deck that will win for him—any queen, jack, ten, seven, six, or five. Four of those cards

are already in his hand, but that still leaves twenty cards to help him, and he will beat you 70 percent of the time. He has one of the monster drawing hands which Omaha players call a "wraparound"—that is, he has the flop surrounded—and a wraparound is one of the most highly prized hands in the game. Omaha, in short, is more of a gambling game than hold 'em, a game in which you call more opening bets because the serious action usually begins after the flop. Hold 'em is subtler, more strategic, and more cunning, and most of the significant maneuvering

takes place before the flop.

That is why Doyle Brunson, twice World Poker Champion and author of *Super/System*, the best and most sophisticated of how-to poker books, called no-limit hold 'em "the Cadillac of poker games." The possibilities and subtleties are infinite. A pair of aces in the hole may be the strongest starting hand, but after the flop everything changes: a small pair in the hole suddenly becomes three of a kind (a set); two connected or suited cards turn into a straight or a flush. The complexities are so great that Brunson devotes two hundred pages to hold 'em—three or four times the space he gives to any other form of poker. The late Johnny Moss, the Grand Old Man of Poker and three times World Champion, once said, "Hold 'em is to stud and draw what chess is to checkers." It is a game of wits and psychology and position, of bluffing, thrust and counterthrust, and it depends less on cards than on skill and character and courage.

Hold 'em has been played in Texas since the end of the nineteenth century. In the first twelve years of the World Series of Poker, four of the nine champions were Texans—Moss, Brunson, "Amarillo Slim" Preston, and the redoubtable Jack Straus—and only two of the others were not Southerners. To play hold 'em well you need the qualities that Texans most admire, the qualities associated with the frontier spirit: bravery, self-reliance, opportunism, and a willingness to take risks. The game took a long time to catch on outside the South, but in the last twenty years hold 'em and Omaha have become the most popular forms of poker, the stuff of champions, and played all over the world. In the pages that follow, hold 'em is the game that will figure most prominently.

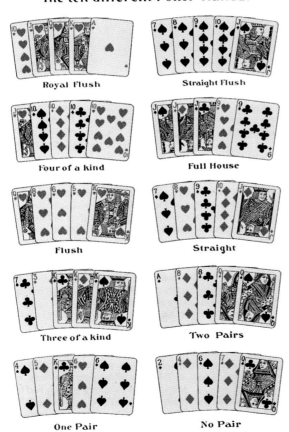

The ten different Poker Hands.

Royal Flush

Straight Flush

Four of a kind

Full House

Flush

Straight

Three of a kind

Two Pairs

One Pair

No Pair

⊗ this page: "The odds are merely a framework for play, like the lines on a tennis court," David Spanier. This page from David Curtis's 1901 book *The Science of Draw Poker* illustrates the ten different hands.

⊗ opposite page: Doyle "Texas Dolly" Brunson, World Champion of 1976 and 1977 and author of the poker book *Super/System*.

CHAPTER 3

CHARACTER *and* COURAGE

Good poker is patience; great poker is courage.

Rick Bennet, *King of a Small World*

⊗ This joker is from a stylish deck designed and published
   by Theodore DeLand circa 1914.

FREDERICK AND STEVEN BARTHELME, writing about their near-fatal addiction to blackjack in *Double Down,* had this to say about the gambler's holy grail, that blissful moment when the five magic symbols come up together on a slot machine and someone hits the jackpot:

That win was just two hundred and fifty dollars, but the money wasn't the point. The perfect thing had happened. The possibility of perfection was something most of our friends and colleagues at the university where we worked no longer believed in. They had grown up, become wise, accepted things as they were. But everybody in the casino believed. However crude, however dizzy, however self-deluded these people may have been, they knew how to hope, how to imagine life as something other than a dreary chore. They imagined that something wonderful might happen, something that could change their lives. This was their fool's secret, one they shared with drunks, artists, and children, all of whom they resembled. Our fellow gamblers were serious, not like academics but in the furious way that children are serious, concentrating on play, oblivious, intense, yet at ease. Essentially they came to the casino to be children [because] gambling is a child's vice practised largely by adults.

Behind every form of gambling, the Barthelme brothers are saying, is this dual ideal of play and perfection combined—an ideal that is as pure, in its complicated way, as the absorption of a child building the ultimate card castle or a poet writing a flawless lyric.

That is what I meant when I called Yardley's style of poker "classical." It might seem an inflated word for a shady pastime, but it is wholly appropriate, for there is a kind of strict beauty in the game when it is played by experts, when every detail is accounted for, and every nuance recognized. The excitement of this style of poker has almost nothing to do with the passive, masochistic thrill of playing the slots or roulette, where you are at the mercy of the random workings of a machine or a rolling ivory ball. It is more like the tension of chess, the most purely intellectual of all games. And at a certain shared level of skill, poker, like chess, is psychological combat. It depends not only on the cards but on your insight into your opponent's state of mind. Is he depressed or riding high? What is his financial position off the table as well as on? What are his vanities, his fears? At its best, poker is a contest of wills and personalities, one end of which is power. You want to be able to predict, even to dictate, how the other players will respond to each of your moves.

To reach that position of power you not only need to have mastered the technical intricacies of the game, you also need to be able to read the other players. "If you really want to know me," they say, "come and

⊗ opposite page: Johnny Moss, "The Grand Old Man of Poker," is shown here in his seventies. Moss won the World Championship in 1970, 1971, and 1974.

guys were close friends, yet I learned that if one of them tugged his ear when he called a bet, it meant he had nothing and was hoping to fill his hand; another always cleared his throat before he bluffed; a third said "raise" when he had you beat and "raise the pot" when he was bluffing. Although I rarely saw any of them away from the table, I knew their nervous tics as well as, or maybe better than, their wives did.

Knowing the other players, however, is less important than knowing yourself. "The first thing a gambler has to do is make friends with himself," said Puggy Pearson, who won the World Series of Poker in 1973. "A lot of people go through the world thinking they're someone else. There are a lot of players sitting at this table with mistaken identities." Making friends with yourself means being able to recognize your own weaknesses—impulsiveness, impatience, greed, fear. But the greatest enemy of all is ego.

The long-running Tuesday game that I called my poker college was kept afloat for years by one player. He helped pay our mortgages and educate our kids, he subsidized our vacations and nights out on the town, and all because of his vanity. He had, heaven knows, something to be vain about. He was a successful wine merchant, a connoisseur of great vintages, and friend of famous wine growers around the world. He also knew a good deal about modern painting, had a nose for original new talent, and a fine collection of pictures. He spoke three languages and even published a couple of bad novels. The one thing he did not know about was poker. He was a dreadful player, a wild gambler who called on anything and ignored the odds because he knew nothing about them. This was in a tough game where we played a lot of wild-card variations—the kind he liked, the kind where crazy gamblers can sometimes get lucky—but we played them skillfully and hard. He didn't stand a chance. Yet he kept coming back for more

play poker with me." It is not enough to study the betting patterns of the other people at the table; you must also analyze their characters—separate the fox from the buffalo, the tortoise from the hare, the rock from the snake beneath it.

And all the while you are watching for "tells," those small, involuntary, or unconscious telltale gestures that indicate tension. That, too, is a science. "Crazy Mike" Caro wrote a whole book about it, and, in *Fast Company*, Jon Bradshaw's loving portrait of professional gamblers, the great Johnny Moss summed up a lifetime's study in these words: "You have to learn what kind of hand this guy shows down, watch that one's moves, watch the veins in his neck, watch his eyes, the way he sweats."

This style of attention creates a curious but impersonal intimacy. In that first Friday night game I played in regularly, for example, none of the other

⊗   The cover of G. Frank Lydston's 1906 book *Poker Jim.*

because he couldn't believe that what he considered to be a gang of layabouts, who lacked his inestimable advantages, could possibly be his superiors in anything. He persuaded himself that he wasn't losing to better players; he was losing because he was unlucky. Despite his education and his airs, he was a surly man without any social graces, a bully who mistook rudeness for charm. The more he lost the ruder he became, but that was fine by us. It is easy to smile at an insult and pretend it's funny when the person insulting you is simultaneously hosing you with money. Whenever he lost too consistently and dropped out of the game, one of the more self-sacrificing players would call him up and invite him to the theater or the opera or a football match. Anything to keep him sweet and keep him playing. It sounds sly, but that's poker. So he kept coming back, losing, dropping out, then coming back again, until he finally graduated to the Great Poker Game in the Sky. Although he ate and drank and smoked too much, and never exercised, he managed to hang on for his allotted biblical span—three score and ten—so maybe he beat the odds in the end. Even so, I suspect he died thinking he'd been unfairly outdrawn.

According to Puggy Pearson, "Losing is like smoking. It's habit-forming." In *The Hustler*, the greatest of all gambling movies, Bert Gordon (George C. Scott) says much the same to the young pool hustler, Fast Eddie Felson (Paul Newman). Fast Eddie has lost his first classic encounter with the reigning pool champion, Minnesota Fats (Jackie Gleason), despite being equally talented and far ahead for most of the game.

"Then, what beat me?" he asks.

Bert Gordon is a professional gambler with alligator blood in his veins. "Character," he replies. "You're a born loser. You have no trouble losing when you have a good excuse. It's one of the best indoor sports, feeling sorry for yourself. A sport enjoyed by all, especially the born loser."

The rest of the movie is about how Fast Eddie acquires character the hard way: first, he has his thumbs broken, then the girl he loves is maneuvered into taking her own life; and Bert Gordon is behind both disasters. Once he has been refined in this fire, Fast Eddie comes back and beats the great Fats.

He has acquired the discipline, hardheadedness, and courage that poker players call "intestinal fortitude" and "heart." The professionals who play in the biggest games in Las Vegas are, by definition, the best poker players in the world—if they weren't, they wouldn't survive in games where tens and sometimes hundreds of thousands of dollars regularly change hands. But they take the science of the game for granted and know that what separates the good players from the truly great is character. "Playing poker for a living gives you backbone," Bobby Baldwin, the World Champion in 1978, once told me. "You cannot survive without that intangible quality we call heart. I don't care how bad you are going or how good, you have to stand solid. Poker is a character builder—especially the bad times. The mark of a top player is not how much he wins when he is winning but how he handles his losses. If you win for thirty days in a row, that makes no difference if on the thirty-first you have a bad night, go crazy, and throw it all away. You can't survive that way. In this business, you have to be able to live with adversity." And that, of course, is precisely the lesson Fast Eddie had to learn the hard way.

Character means different things to different people. This is how Puggy Pearson described his version of it to Jon Bradshaw:

"A gambler's ace is his ability to think clearly under stress. That's very important, because, you see, fear is the basis of all mankind. In cards, you psyche 'em out, you shark 'em, you put the fear of God in 'em. That's life. Everything's mental in life. The butt was made to lug the mind around. The most important thing in gamblin' is knowing the sixty-forty end of the proposition and knowing the human element. Some folks may know one of 'em, but ain't many know 'em both. I believe in logics. Cut and dried.

Two and two ain't nothing in this world but four. But them suckers always think it's somethin' different . . . I play percentages in everything. Now, knowing the percentages perfectly, the kind of numbers you read in them books, is all right, but the hidden percentages are more important. The real thing to know is that folks will stand to lose more than they will to win. That's the most important percentage there is. I mean, if they lose, they're willing to lose everything. If they win, they're usually satisfied to

⊗ above: "Puggy" Pearson, World Champion of 1973.

⊗ opposite page: Puggy Pearson poses with his van. In Jon Bradshaw's words, "The true professional gambler was an outlaw, a truant travelling along back roads."

win enough to pay for dinner and a show. The best gamblers know that.

"Everything's mental in life. The butt was made to lug the mind around." Puggy was brought up dirt poor in the hollows of northern Tennessee, and he left school at fourteen, so he had every right to be proud of his innate talent for "logics." But making a spectacular living out of knowing the percentages was only a small part of the pleasure he derived from being a gambling man:

Gambling isn't the money, you know. I've been broke lots of times. That don't mean nothing. It's the competition. It's laying your ability on the line and invitin' challenge. That's all I can do. I do it for myself. That's what I take pride in—being a winner. That's what life's all about, ain't it? It's the satisfaction of performing well. That's all you ever get if you're smart. Just a little self-satisfaction and enjoyment. And that's enough. Why hell, there ain't a breeze in the sky floats freer than I do.

The man who floated freest of all the top poker professionals was Jack Straus, who won the World Championship in 1982 and died six years later during a marathon high-stakes poker game in Los Angeles. Straus was the epitome of the gambling man—charming, witty, debonair, and a great raconteur, a man who was willing to wager crazy sums of money on any proposition if he thought he had an edge. (He once bet $100,000 on the outcome of a high school basketball game.) He was fearless when he gambled and, like his colleagues, he judged players as he himself wished to be judged—not by their mathematical skill in reckoning the odds but by their "intestinal fortitude." "I wouldn't pay a ten-year-old kid a dime an hour to sit in a low-stakes game and wait for the nuts," he once told me. "If there's no risk in losing, there's no high in winning. I have only a limited amount of time on this earth, and I want to live every second of it. That's why I'm willing to play anyone in the world for any amount. It doesn't matter who they are. Once they have a hundred or two hundred thousand dollars' worth of chips in front of them, they all look the same. They all look like dragons to me, and I want to slay them."

Straus discovered his talent for cards at high school. At sixteen he won a car in a poker game, which the loser had to deliver to his home because Straus hadn't yet learned to drive. He was also a natural athlete and because of his exceptional height—he was six foot seven inches, hence his nickname, "Treetops"—he was a college basketball star at Texas A & M, where he took a degree in physical education. Like many of the other professionals, he turned to poker for the competition when his physical powers began to diminish. He once told me that when he played basketball he suffered from a nervous stomach that prevented him from eating or sleeping if his team lost. "Poker's the same," he went on. "It's all about competition. Different people are afraid of different things. Me, I'm afraid of embarrassment. If I lose, I don't give a damn about the money, but I just hate the embarrassment of being beaten."

Straus's will to win, coupled with his fearlessness and extraordinary psychological insight, made him a devastating opponent at the poker table, particularly in short-handed games. He was less effective in tournament play where, in the early stages, patience is at a premium. It was typical of his particular talent that, when he won the World Series, he had been down to his last $500 on the first day, then bluffed his way back from the dead and went on to win the title and $520,000. It was also typical of his two-fisted generosity that he kept the half million and gave the odd $20,000 to the dealers and the card-room staff.

Like all the top players, Straus had a total disregard for money, except as an instrument he used in the poker game. "Chips don't have a home," he used to say. He also said, "If money is your god, you can forget no-limit poker because it's going to hurt you too much to turn loose of it. The way I feel about those pieces of green paper is, you can't take them with you and they may not have much value in five years' time, but right now I can take them and trade them in for pleasure, or to bring pleasure to other people. If they'd have wanted you to hold on to money, they'd have made it with handles on."

Straus was a master of tall stories, mostly about himself, often featuring his indifference to money, and all beginning "Did I ever tell you about the time when . . . ?" The most outrageous of them was about the time when the IRS brought him to court, saying he owed the government $3,000,000. Straus was flat broke at the time and knew there was no way he could ever pay up. When the black day of his trial came, he arrived in court early and sat at the back with his lawyer, waiting for his case to be called,

⊗ opposite page: Jack Straus, World Champion of 1982.

⊗ above: An array of mid-19th-century hand-scrimshawed mother-of-pearl chips.

⊗ opposite page: "The winner is not the player who wins the most pots. The winner is the player who wins the most money," Anthony Holden. Jack Straus is seen here after winning the World Championship in 1982.

while the judge listened to another offender who owed $35,000 in back taxes. "Your honor," the man was saying, "I'm an honest guy. Give me a little time. Let me pay it off, plus interest, over five years. If you don't do that, the only way I can settle up is by selling my house. Then what will happen to my wife and kids? We'll be on the street, your honor. It'll break up our lives." When Straus heard that, he told me, "I was so plumb sorry for the poor guy that I stood up at the back of the court and said, 'Your honor, just stick it on my tab!'"

Straus's utter disregard for money is best illustrated by a true story that has gone into gambling legend. Back in 1970, a terrible run at the poker tables in Las Vegas reduced him to his last $40. Instead of quitting, he took the $40 to the blackjack table and bet it all on a single hand. He won and continued to bet all the money in front of him until he had turned the $40 into $500. He took the $500 back to the poker table and ran it up to $4,000, returned to the blackjack table and transformed the $4,000 into $10,000. He then bet the whole sum on the Kansas City Chiefs in the Super Bowl and won $20,000. In less than twenty-four hours, he went from near bankruptcy to relative affluence, but that is not the point of the story. The point is his refusal to compromise. Each time he bet, he bet all the money he had, from the first $40 to the final $10,000. As Damon Runyon wrote of Sky Masterson, the hero of *Guys and Dolls*, "He will bet all he has, and nobody can bet more than this."

Straus was fearless, but he wasn't reckless. He knew how to hunker down, tighten up, and endure the bad runs. They, too, are dues the professional gambler pays for being outside the system. He once told me that his father, whom he loved, had worked hard all his life—he was the manager of a packing plant—in the expectation of enjoying his leisure when he retired at sixty-five. But he died when he was fifty-eight "and never got to go anywhere or do anything." Straus took that lesson to heart and resolved to live his own life on his own terms.

Straus was also a marksman, a crack shot, and when he wasn't playing poker he went hunting, a recreation he pursued all over the globe, like Hemingway, the author he most admired. The first time he shot a lion in Africa he had the paw of the beast mounted and on it, inscribed in gold, his favorite proverb: "Better one day as a lion than a hundred years as a lamb." It is a motto all the great poker players would subscribe to, and it is born out of that courage, self-knowledge, and indifference to adversity that sets them as free as a breeze in the sky.

CHAPTER 4

Money: THE LANGUAGE *of* POKER

A good gambler can get money out of a lamp post.

In poker, money is power.

Titanic Thompson

⊗ opposite page: W. C. Fields in a poker scene from
Universal Pictures' 1939 movie *My Little Chickadee.*

IN *MY LITTLE CHICKADEE,* someone asks W. C. Fields if poker is a game of chance. He answers, "Not the way I play it." He was speaking as a cardsharp, but he was also speaking the truth. As I said earlier, serious poker is no more about gambling than rock climbing is about taking risks. Both are risky activities, of course, and accidents sometimes happen to the canniest experts.

Climbers misjudge the weather or the solidity of the rock or the difficulty of a move or the limits of their strength; and when they do the consequences may be painful—frostbite, a broken limb, a broken neck. Similarly, even the best poker players must endure terrible runs of cards when nothing goes right and every good hand is outdrawn: "In the long run there's no luck in poker," Rick Bennet wrote sourly, "but the short run is longer than most people know." But in poker, as in climbing, the point of the game is to develop enough skill to minimize the element of chance.

Repeat: minimize, not eliminate. Chess is a game of pure information, like poker with all the cards exposed; the better player will *always* win; that is why a computer can be programmed to play it so well. But the only way a computer could be made to play top-level poker would be by introducing a randomizing factor into the program that would correspond both to the element of bluff and to the random way the cards fall. The better player will usually win at poker, but because the cards are shuffled and dealt haphazardly the sucker occasionally gets lucky and

beats the expert—occasionally though not for long. According to Terence Reece, a great cardplayer who played bridge for England, there is nothing to choose between bridge and poker in terms of skill. Yet that's not how the uninitiated—or the suckers—see it. For example, before the British Parliament passed the Gaming Act, in 1960, it was illegal to play poker in a card club, because whichever bureaucracy controlled these matters had officially classified it, along with bingo, craps, and roulette, as a game of chance. I suppose the civil servants were confused, as they often are, by the appearance of the game, rather than its reality. Poker looks like gambling—and at a low level it is gambling—because it has to be played for money.

Playing for money, however, means two different things, depending on whether the emphasis is on "playing" or "money." This, for example, is how David Sklansky begins the first chapter of his book *Poker Theory*, and the italics are his: "When we play, we must realize, before anything else, that we are *out to make money*." Sklansky is a Las Vegas–based expert, and his books are bibles for small-time hustlers who

grind out a living in low-stakes games and reckon their success by their hourly earning rate: if they can come out a bet and a half ahead each hour—$30 in a $10–$20-limit game—then they are making a satisfactory living. This is subsistence poker and it is geared to what Sklansky calls "positive expectation": extracting the maximum return from the very few unbeatable hands a player might expect to get in any session.

This is a businessman's attitude to poker, the small-minded, remorseless style that Jack Straus dis-

missed when he said, "I wouldn't pay a ten-year-old kid a dime an hour to sit in a low stakes game and wait for the nuts." He called it, contemptuously, "a disciplined job," adding, "Anyone who wants to work out the mathematics can be a limit player and chisel out an existence. You just have to discipline yourself to sit there and wait." Mickey Appleman, another high roller, though not in Straus's league, put it more romantically: "Certain individuals come here just to make money," he said. "They grind, grind, grind in the small-stakes games, they make a living and they

⊗ The formidable players in this poker game include David Sklansky (leaning on table) and Jack Straus (seated).

have no down side. But they have no gamble in them, either, so they will never know the enjoyment of the high roller, the romance of gambling. Poker playing is strictly a business to these small-stakes players, but to the high rollers it's a business and also a pleasure; it's fun, it's a game, it's gamesmanship. After all, what are we all here for at the Horseshoe? When you are playing for hundreds of thousands of dollars, it's not the money. I mean, how much do you need? It's the gamesmanship, the competition, the thrill of letting it all hang out. Poker for big money is a high-risk sport, like driving a racing car."

What Appleman is describing is a polar difference in temperament. Straus was an artist and an adventurer at the poker table, a man with a huge natural talent for the game who loved playing the finest of fine lines instead of waiting for those rare, unbeatable hands that gamblers call "the stone-cold nuts." Sklansky, in contrast, is a mathematician with a flair for statistics and probabilities and an unusual ability for analyzing the odds on the spot, as the cards turn. On one level both of them would have agreed: the art of playing well is to make the most out of your good cards and lose the least on the less good. Where they differed was in the mind-set which, in the course of the game, translates poker chips into real money, the kind you use to pay the rent, to buy food and drink, to lead a life. And that is something the top players never do.

According to Chip Reese, who is generally considered to be one of the best all-round players in the world, "Money means nothing. If you really cared about it you wouldn't be able to sit down at a poker table and bluff off fifty thousand dollars. If I thought what that could buy me, I could not be a good player. Money is just the yardstick by which you measure your success. In Monopoly, you try to win all the cash by the end of the game. It's the same in poker: you treat chips like play money and don't think about

it until it's all over." As it happens, Reese was speaking truer than he knew. I once played in an impromptu game in London. The stakes were serious, but we had no chips, so the host filched his son's Monopoly set and we used the bills at their face value.

This ability to immunize yourself from the real value of money, to treat the chips as what A. J. Meyers, another top player, called "just a bag of beans," explains the curious and—to the newcomer—disconcerting Las Vegas custom of dropping the zeroes from bets. The first time I played in a pot-limit hold 'em game in Vegas, I bet $50 after the flop and was disconcerted

⊗ above: Chip Reese, captured here in contemplation, is widely considered to be among the world's best poker players.

⊗ opposite page: Money is the language of poker.

when the dealer said "A nickel to play." Two players called. A cowboy sitting across the table eyed me, eyed my stack, then, without seeming to count them, separated twelve green $25 chips from the pile in front of him and growled, "Raise it up a quarter." "A quarter to you," the dealer said. When I looked puzzled, he explained patiently, as though to a dumb child, "Two hundred and fifty dollars, sir."

This was my first lesson in the Las Vegas truth that chips have only a relative value; they are merely a convenient way of keeping score. According to the size of the game, a "nickel" is $5 or $50 or $500, a "dime" is $10 or $100 or $1,000, and when the whales bet a "big dime" in their giant games, they mean $10,000. If you ask them why they use this shorthand, they will usually answer, "It makes things simpler." But what they are really doing is expressing their indifference to money as the rest of the world sees it.

This is a universal procedure among high rollers, although they take it further in Las Vegas—the only town on earth, they say, which makes you think a $100 bill won't buy a loaf of bread. The pros wander around with great wads of those bills stuffed in their pockets—fifty bills to a wad and each wad casually held together with elastic bands—but few of them carry small change. Lesser bills seem below the level

⊗ top left and bottom right: This hand-scrimshawed ivory poker chip, circa 1870, is believed to have been used either to commemorate the Mississippi riverboat *Robert E. Lee* or to gamble on board.

⊗ top right: This mid-19th-century hand-scrimshawed ivory poker chip is believed to have belonged to a wealthy Western judge.

⊗ bottom left: A mid-19th-century hand-scrimshawed ivory poker chip.

of their attention, mere trifles they use for tips, though sometimes, when the heat is really on, they even tip in hundreds. During one gigantic game at Binion's Horseshoe, Jimmy Chagra, a drug baron who was in town for a final fling while he unsuccessfully appealed against a thirty-year sentence in Leavenworth Penitentiary, tipped a cocktail waitress $10,000 when she brought him a complimentary bottle of Mountain Valley water. Similarly, when the photographer Ulvis Alberts was at the World Series in 1980, shooting the wonderfully atmospheric portraits of players which he published in his book *Poker Faces*, some of the contestants asked him for prints. He tried charging them $75, but "suddenly there was a problem," he told me. "Nobody had change. So I charged them $100 and everyone was happy."

The idea that poker is a game that has to be played for money, therefore, means two different things, according to temperament. For the "rocks," who bet only on certainties and treat the game as a source of steady income, money is always money. For the more creative players, who are not necessarily more reckless but know better how to calibrate the risks they take, money is a tool of their trade, like a wrench to a plumber, and chips are just a way of keeping score. According to Eric Drache, "The trick is to look on chips as units. It doesn't matter whether it costs you $500 a bet or $5, the odds remain the same."

Chips, however, have a third and more profound significance in poker: they combine with the cards to form the very language of the game. What you do with your chips—when and how you bet or check or raise—is a form of communication. You ask subtle questions with them and receive subtle answers. The questions and answers may be misleading—a big bet might be a sign of weakness, an attempt to drive the other players out of the pot because you do not have the hand you purport to have—but the combination

of cards and money and position at the table creates a complex pattern of information (or illusion) that controls the flow of the game. In poker, betting and what is called "money management"—knowing when to call or raise or fold so that your bankroll is never fatally depleted—are as much an art as reading the cards and reckoning the odds.

This is true, above all, in no-limit hold 'em where a player can bet as much as he wants, regardless of the size of the pot. One of the masters of this game is Crandall Addington, an elegantly bearded Texan who used to set the sartorial standards for the World Series—a mink Stetson, silk shirts, suits of fine linen, and Dior ties he never loosened no matter how long he played. Addington is an amateur who made his

⊗ Texan poker master Crandall Addington added elegance
   to the game.

millions in oil and real estate and doesn't play for the money, but he is a fearsome competitor. "Limit poker is a science, but no-limit is an art," he once said. "In limit, you are shooting at a target. In no-limit, the target comes alive and shoots back at you."

I began to understand what he meant by that when I heard him discussing a no-limit hold 'em hand with a friend. The friend had been dealt ace-ten of hearts and had called a raise from someone sitting in an early position. The flop was a black king and two low hearts, a six and a deuce; there was $2,000 in the pot. An early raise before the flop usually indicates that the player is holding an ace and a king. Sure enough, the man came out betting.

"How much?" Addington asked.

"The pot," said the friend. "Two thousand dollars."

"So what did you do?"

"I just flat called him."

"Wrong," said Addington. "You should have raised him fifteen thousand and let him think about it."

If he had been made to think about it, what deductions would the other player have drawn from the huge raise? Would he have been able to put Addington's friend on a drawing hand? What kind of four flusher would dare to bet so much? Wouldn't he rather have thought that the raiser had a pair in his hand—two deuces, two sixes, even two kings—cards that gave him a set (three of a kind) and thereby made his own ace-king almost worthless? When the target starts shooting back the marksman is in trouble.

Here is another example of the fierce but subtle language of poker that uses chips as a form of communication. I described this hand in *The Biggest Game in Town*, and it was played in what was, without any doubt, the biggest game in Las Vegas while I was there in 1981. It was a cash game strictly for the heavy hitters. Doyle Brunson, Jack Straus, Puggy Pearson, and Crandall Addington were sitting around

the table, along with Jesse Alto, a car dealer from Houston famous for his stamina—he once played for a whole week without taking a break. The atmosphere was mellow, but the stakes were high. The boys were playing a little poker together, wisecracking, needling, and outsmarting one another from behind mountains of chips and banded wads of $100 bills. No one had sat down with less than $50,000.

Before the flop, Alto raised the opening bet, then called when he was modestly reraised by Straus. The other players folded. The flop came king, ten, eight, all of different suits. Alto, who had a king and eight of diamonds in the hole, checked to trap Straus. Straus paused, then bet $1,000—again, modestly by the standards of the game, but large enough for a bluff. This was what Alto had been hoping for; with his two pairs, kings and eights, he raised $5,000.

Straus slumped even further in his chair. He always sat hunched at the table, shoulders forward, curly gray head and curly gray beard sunk between them, as though denying his great height. As I mentioned earlier, away from the poker table as well as at it, Straus was a big-game hunter and he had marksman's eyes: dark blue, slanting down from right to left, the left eye always slightly closed, like a man taking aim. He watched Alto in silence for a long time, but Alto did not stir. Then Straus cupped his hands around his cards and squeezed them slightly upward with his thumbs. Another pause. Then quickly, almost fretfully, he pushed several stacks of chips into the center.

The dealer counted them carefully and said, "Raise thirty thousand dollars."

The target had come alive and was shooting back.

Alto did not move, but his erect back seemed to curve infinitesimally, as if under the pressure of a great weight. He sat considering the alternatives while Puggy Pearson lit a giant cigar. Did Straus have a king and an ace in the hole, or even two pairs, like

Alto himself? Or did he have a pair that gave him, with the flop, a set of kings or tens or eights? Or did he have a queen and a jack in the hole and was betting "on the come," hoping to complete a straight? Or, since this was Jack Straus, the master of the withering bluff and a man with a reputation for total fearlessness, was he simply bluffing?

For long, empty minutes, the two players faced each other across the table, unmoving and unspeaking, like figures in stone. Finally, Alto counted out his chips and pushed them gloomily forward. Straus's bet had set him in for all his money, so there would be no more betting. He turned over his king and eight. Straus nodded, and then, in a matter-of-fact way, turned over his hole cards: two tens. The ten in the center had given him a set of three, and only another king could save Alto. The dealer burned—discarded—the top card and dealt a seven, burned the next card and dealt a four. The three tens were good.

In hold 'em at this level, the target does not just shoot back, it also shifts about like a will-o'-the-wisp, maneuvering for position. In the previous hour, Straus had twice bet in precisely the same pattern, but with weaker cards; both times, Alto had called him and won. The only difference was that the sums involved had been much smaller—a couple of thousand rather than tens of thousands. I had watched those two earlier hands uncomprehending, for it seemed—even to an outsider and a relative novice like me—that Straus was betting on losing cards. Yet I was also aware that if I knew it so did he, since one of the many gifts that separates the professionals from the amateurs is the ability to read their opponents' hands with uncanny accuracy from the tiniest clues: timing, position, the way their fingers move their chips or their eyes flicker, even the pulse beat in their neck. Like all the top professionals, Straus had that unnerving clairvoyance and had played for so long, and with such concentra-

tion, that nothing was new to him or unfamiliar or unfathomable. Yet there he was, apparently throwing away his money as carelessly as any tyro. I was wrong, of course. Straus had been setting Alto up for the kill, raising his confidence, lulling him into the belief that he, Straus, was playing loosely, so that when his moment came he could make the same ploy with a monster hand and Alto would call him. The two losing hands were investments that finally yielded a disproportionate return—$8,000 to make $40,000.

Twenty years ago $40,000 was enough to support an average family for a year in comfort. Granted, average wage earners don't play high-stakes poker. Of the millions of poker players in America, only a few thousand ever graduate to the games at Binion's and, of them, not more than a dozen or two would stand a chance in the really big games. Even so, the normal regard for money seems to be on hold in poker games, especially during tournaments, when amateurs from private games in the prosperous suburbs—businessmen, lawyers, rich doctors, and orthodontists—flood into town for the action. They breeze into the bigger games, call every raise, play their half-decent hands too strongly, drop a couple of grand, then race back into the casino to try to recoup their losses at craps or blackjack. They are noisy, cheerful, and intermittently aggressive, but they seem not quite to know what is happening from one minute to the next. There is a bullish, head-down urgency about them, and their eyes are unfocused. All they want to do is cram as much action as they can into the time they have stolen from their routine lives and their families. They are men with a mission, running on adrenaline, pursuing some impossible mirage, and, for them, money is beside the point. What matters is the thrill of action. Their Western equivalents are the cattle ranchers and wildcatters, the good ol' boys who roll into town to whoop it up a little and just loo-ove raising and reraising with second-best cards into those unbeatable hands that Sklansky and his friends wait all night for. All of them are grist to the professionals' mill, and they keep the poker economy running.

"This town hypnotizes people," Doyle Brunson told me. "Guys who won't bet $20 at home come out here and bet $500 or $1,000 without even thinking—particularly during the poker tournament. It's like being inside a pressure cooker. If you're not careful, you reach boiling point and explode. Then you just throw your money away. They keep hammering and hammering at you, until you lose touch with reality about everything." Poker in Las Vegas is like a speeded-up experiment in evolution. Players from all over the globe beat their local games, then come into town and lose their money to the local experts.

A few grand up or down means nothing much to the wealthy amateurs, though their wives might not agree. Indeed, even the wives of the top professionals sometimes find it hard to adjust to the insane world their husbands take for granted. Eric Drache told me that his wife, Jane, once called him in the middle of a game to say she'd been in a car accident. The conversation went like this:

Eric:	"Are you hurt?"
Jane:	"No."
Eric:	"Is anyone else hurt?"
Jane:	"No."
Eric:	"That's all right then."
Jane:	"But I've done $1,500 worth of damage to the side of the car."
Eric:	"Then call the insurance."
Jane:	"But $1,500 damage to our beautiful Jaguar!"
Eric:	"Honey, I'm stuck four beautiful Jaguars at this moment. Call the insurance."

The wives are living in the real world of groceries and clothes and dentists' bills, whereas the husbands are temporarily in a dreamland where play's the thing and money isn't quite real. It doesn't even look real. Instead of a green treasury bill validated by a president's face, it's a colored disk stamped with a number and the name of a casino. Chips, in fact, are the currency of Las Vegas. When a gambler arranges a line of credit with a casino, he takes the money in chips. You tip with them, pay for meals and drinks and sex with them, and could probably buy goods with them in stores. The better adjusted to them you become, the further reality recedes. To eat a slap-up meal with all the trimmings and pay for it with a couple of battered green discs is no longer a business transaction, it is magic.

The poker chip is like a conjuror's sleight of hand that turns an egg into a billiard ball, a necessity of life into a plaything, reality into illusion. People who freeze up at the sight of a hundred-dollar bill, thinking it could buy them a week's food at the supermarket, will toss a black chip into the pot without even hesitating if the odds are right. "Chips don't have a home," said Jack Straus. "People will play much higher with chips than they will with cash. For some reason, it is harder for inferior players to turn loose of money, but give them chips and they get caught up, mesmerized by the game." A New York gambler who goes by the name of Big Julie put it best when he remarked sagely, "The guy who invented gambling was bright, but the guy who invented the chip was a genius."

⊗ opposite page: These mid-19th-century hand-scrimshawed ivory poker chips are from an old Western saloon called El Dorado.

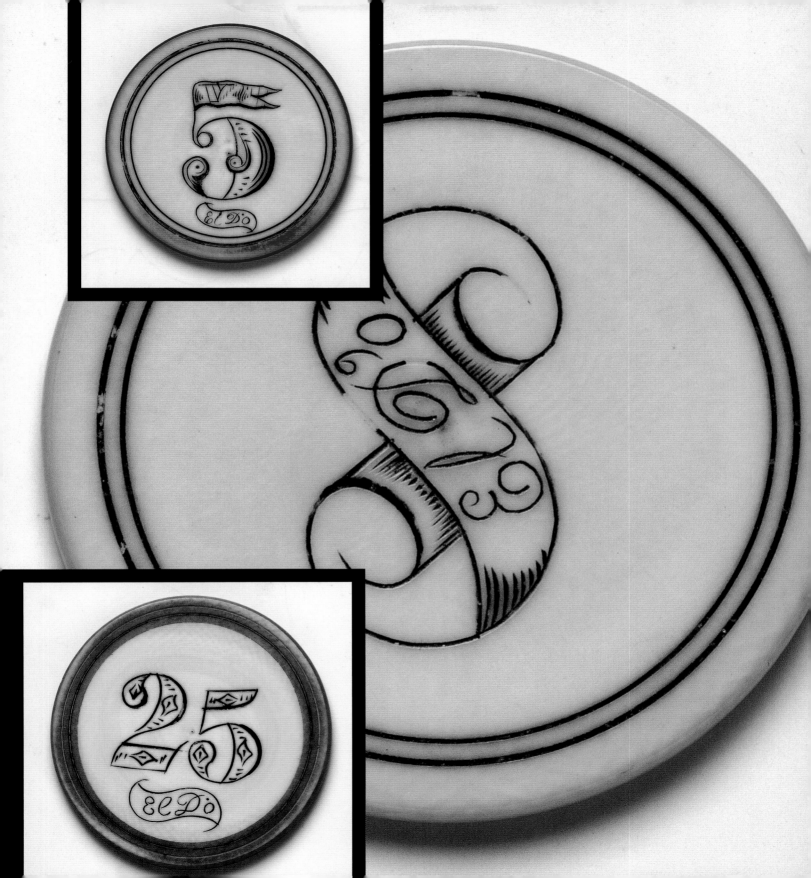

BL*U*FF

The nature of it is, that you are to endeavour to impose upon the judgment of the rest that play, and particularly on the person that chiefly offers to oppose you, by boasting of cards in your hand, whether Pair Royals, Pairs, or others that you are better than his or hers that play against you.

Richard Seymour, on brag, in *The Compleat Gamester* (1725)

⊗ This mid-19th-century glass ambrotype pictures men playing
   poker. It was uncommon to find images of men playing poker
   during this period.

BLUFFING, BRAGGING, BOASTING that the cards in your hand are better than those in your opponent's and then putting your money where your mouth is, is as old as the game itself. Older, in fact, since bluff was intrinsic to the European vying games — English brag, French bouillotte or poque, German pochen, Italian primero — from which American poker developed. The difference is that poker is a more sophisticated game than its predecessors and bluffing is a proportionately more sophisticated skill.

Not always, of course, and certainly not in the early days of the game. One of the first and most famous recorded bluffs took place in Washington, D.C., where poker always seems to have been the recreational game of choice — perhaps because it so closely resembles the game of politics. (George Washington himself played regularly, though none too successfully, and kept detailed accounts of his wins and losses.) The players were Henry Clay and Daniel Webster, the game was draw, and the hand has gone into poker history. This is how David Spanier described it in his book *Total Poker*:

With Webster dealing, Clay drew one card on the draw and Webster stood pat. The two went on raising each other until each had $2,000 on the table. At this stage Clay stopped reraising and called. According to this account Webster laughed sheep-ishly and threw down his cards. "I only have a pair of deuces," he said. Clay laughed too. "The pot is yours," he said. "I only have an ace high."

In the early days of the nineteenth century, $2,000 was a fortune, so what made these two shrewd operators go on raising and reraising each other? The only answer can be that each somehow sensed that the other was weak, that each had some small, unconscious physical tell — a flicker of the eyelid, an odd inflection of the voice, a slight hesitation when he handled his chips — that showed the other player that the pat hand and the one-card draw were both bluffs. Clay and Webster were hard, ambitious men as well as fearless gamblers, and when they faced each other head-to-head their pride was on the line. Each smelled the other's weakness and was determined not to blink.

Paul Newman runs the same crazy bluff in the

movie *Cool Hand Luke*, raising and reraising a five-card stud hand with a bare king showing and nothing in the hole. Unlike Henry Clay, Luke does not falter, his opponent eventually folds his stronger hand, and Luke earns his prison nickname. "Sometimes," he says, "nothing is a pretty cool hand."

The most spectacular bluff of all was also played out in Washington, although it wasn't in a poker game, and it didn't succeed. Richard Nixon was a talented poker player, like his predecessors in the presidency, Truman and Eisenhower. All of them were regular winners, though Ike gave up the game while he was still in the army because he was too tenderhearted: "When I found officers around me losing more than they could afford," he said, "I stopped." Truman went on playing as a relaxation from the burdens of high

⊗ Paul Newman bluffs in this poker scene from the 1967
Warner Brothers' movie *Cool Hand Luke.*

⊗ top left: Despite his Quaker upbringing, Richard Nixon, seen here in 1957, took up poker during his naval service and turned out to be a talented player.

⊗ bottom left: Harry Truman was another White House poker player who used the game to relieve the tensions of high office.

⊗ top right: Dwight Eisenhower also played poker, though his scruples about winning money from his fellow officers led him to give up the game while still in the army.

office—most famously with the White House press corps on board the cruiser *Augusta*, while he was deciding whether or not to drop the atom bomb on Hiroshima. He and his secretary of state, James F. Byrnes, disagreed violently on the decision, and Truman used his—literally—floating poker game to shut Byrnes out. According to Merriman Smith, the United Press correspondent who played in the week-long marathon, Truman "was running a straight stud filibuster against his own Secretary of State."

Nixon was an altogether tougher proposition, although he had been brought up as a Quaker and had never gambled before he joined the navy. But he was also an ambitious young man with a career to make for himself and very little money to make it with, so when he saw the amount of loose cash that was thrown around on the poker tables at the Officers' Club he decided to forgo his religious principles and learn the game. He turned out to be a natural. In *The Real Nixon*, James Udall, who served with him in the Pacific, says: "Nick was as good a poker player as, if not better than, anyone we had ever seen. He played a quiet game, but wasn't afraid of taking chances. He wasn't afraid of running a bluff. Sometimes the stakes were pretty big, but Nick had daring and a flair for knowing what to do." By the time the war ended, he had earned a considerable sum, enough to finance the campaign that got him elected to Congress. His fellow Quakers might not have approved, but at least he had the blessing of Dr. Albert Upton, one of his teachers at Whittier College, California, who said proudly of his ex-pupil, "A man who couldn't hold a hand in a first-class poker game is not fit to be President of the United States." As it happens, Nixon played less as he climbed higher, and when he became Eisenhower's vice-president he stopped altogether. But he never lost his poker player's mentality and in the end it was his undoing.

Spanier calls the Watergate cover-up "the biggest bluff that Nixon ever ran":

The basis of [it] was that if the full weight and prestige of the Presidency were committed to the cover-up, Congress would not "see". . . The bluff itself was not entirely misconceived; after all, the White House had the immense advantage of running the game, so to speak, and of exercising its control over the principal players. The bluff failed in the end because the hands were recorded in the form of tapes. That was why the cover-up was ultimately exposed. If the tapes had been destroyed instead of being doctored, the probability is that Congress would not have nerved itself to bring in a Bill of Impeachment, and Richard Nixon's greatest bluff would have "held."

This is a shrewd analysis, but wrong, I think, in one detail: Congress only got into the game late, when the bluff was already out of hand. At the start Nixon's opponents were merely a couple of hack reporters from the *Washington Post* who would, he thought, easily be intimidated. It was as though, in a game of five-card stud, Nixon was showing ace, king, queen, and jack of spades but had a worthless card of a different suit in the hole. He bet $1,000,000, and the *Washington Post* called him with nothing better than a pair of wired deuces. In other words, Nixon bet the presidency and was seen. It was an insane call, but then journalists are notoriously poor poker players. Maybe Nixon would have known this if he had played with them as often as President Truman did. But he loathed the press as much as they loathed him, and he overrated their poker skills. The Watergate cover-up is the prime example of the old poker maxim "Never try to bluff a mug."

In the hands of an expert, bluff is the subtlest of instruments. When Crandall Addington told his friend he should have raised massively, even though the friend was sure he was losing at that moment, the move Addington was suggesting was not altogether a bluff. The friend had four hearts to the nut flush and, with two cards still to come, he had a 35 percent chance of making his hand. By calling his opponent's $2,000 bet and raising $15,000, he was offering him the wrong odds: the opponent had only contributed at most $3,000 to the pot; another $15,000 to win $21,000 is not a good proposition. In other words, bluff has less to do with bullying and blarney than with percentages and fine judgment.

Mostly it is about reading the other players' cards. This is particularly true in hold 'em, where a great deal depends on the kicker, the side card to the high card in your hand. Ace-king, that is, will always beat ace-queen when the communal cards help neither player or include an ace but not a queen. Addington explained it to me this way: "If you reraise a raiser and he doesn't raise you back, you know he has kicker problems. After that, if an ace falls and he checks to you, it doesn't matter what you've got in your hand; you are playing his cards rather than yours."

This ability to play the other players' cards is the fine art that separates the best players from the less talented. One of the greatest masters of it was Jack Straus, as I myself witnessed when I was writing *The Biggest Game in Town*. The occasion was the final of a World Series event, and the game was ace-to-the-five (no-limit) low ball, a particularly brutal version of draw poker in which conventionally strong hands—like threes of a kind and full houses—are worthless; aces count low, and the perfect, unbeatable hand is a small straight—ace, two, three, four, five—called "the wheel."

It was the closing stage of the tournament, and Straus was head-to-head with Mickey Perry, another Texan. The cards had been running in Perry's favor, and Straus seemed to be playing defensively, surren-

dering the antes with uncharacteristic docility whenever Perry bet. The television cameras moved in and out, the lights blazed, the crowd at the rail jostled and craned to see the action.

Finally, a big hand began to build. Perry bet $1,000 after the deal, and Straus raised him $3,000. There was a long pause. "When he thinks about it like that," Straus told me afterward, "I reckon he's drawing to a nine, maybe a good nine—two, three, four, nine, with some rubbish card." After great hesitation, Perry saw the $3,000 raise and drew one card, as though to demonstrate that Straus had read him accurately. Straus stood pat. The dealer dealt a card to Perry, who shuffled it into his hand and then, holding his cards almost flat against his chest, as though he were chronically nearsighted, squeezed them cautiously out into a fan. Again he checked. Without hesitation, Straus bet $27,000—about three times the amount in the pot. There was another agonized pause, this one far longer than before. "Now I know what he's got," Straus told me. "He's made his nine, but it's rough. He's got a nine-eight." The crowd at the rail fell silent; even the television cameramen covering the event were still. Slowly, reluctantly, Perry separated $27,000 from the other chips in front of him: two and a half stacks of $500 chips, twenty to a stack, and four further five-hundreds—a squat gray mass like a crusader's castle. He waited, calculating how many chips that left him with, and waited again while he peered over at Straus's stacks to see how much he had remaining. Then, even more slowly and reluctantly, he pushed the $27,000 into the center and turned his cards over. They were exactly as Straus had reckoned: two, three, four, eight, nine. Straus tossed his cards facedown into the discards, conceding the hand.

The television director moved forward immediately. "Mr. Straus," he asked, "for the sake of the viewing audience, may we see your cards?"

⊗ opposite page top: These 1910 illustrations add a note of humor to the game.

OPENING A JACK POT

COPYRIGHT 1910 BY S.M.SALKE.

THREE OF A KIND BEATS TWO PAIR

COPYRIGHT 1910 BY S.M.SALKE.

Straus had been, as usual, hunched in his seat, as if to conceal his enormous height. He uncoiled himself a little, reached for the cards, and turned them over slowly, one by one, his face as solemn as a hired mourner's at a wake: queen, queen, queen, jack, jack.

As one man, the railbirds burst into applause.

They were applauding his style, his daring, his dead-eye reckoning of the other man's weaknesses, and whatever else goes to make the romantic image of the gambling man, the misfit whose code of honor and quirky sense of pride make it hard for him to hack it in the straight world, so he prefers to live on the shadowy edge where outlaws and respectable folk intersect. Twenty years ago, that dubious but romantic borderline quality was part of Las Vegas's allure. Before the town cleaned up its act and became just another Disneyland, with pirate battles, jousting knights, exploding volcanoes for the kids, and gambling on the side to keep their parents happy, its gaming tables were the only places where straight citizens could rub shoulders with gangsters and not get into trouble. The

⊗ below: Gamblers favored guns like this 1870 American Colt Firearm second-model Derringer because it was easily concealed and they could carry more than one.

⊗ right: A poker scene from Paramount Pictures' 1957 movie *Gunfight at the O.K. Corral.*

⊗ Marlon Brando in a scene from Paramount Pictures' 1959
Western *Onė-Eyed Jacks*.

wise guys were as much a part of the town's nonstop pageant as the cascades of neon.

The gamblers sat down with the gangsters and usually took their money, but when the Texans ruled the roost in Vegas poker they thought of themselves in different terms—as the last of the cowboys, the true inheritors of the myth of the brave outlaw as it is purveyed in Western movies. The cowboy hero is always a loner, a laconic, honorable man who knows how to handle himself in tight situations, to stand up to bullies and call their bluff. He is also a poker player—rarely a professional, Doc Holliday apart, but good enough to play with the professionals and face them down when they cheat. "Sir, I really like poker," says Henry Fonda's Wyatt Earp in *My Darling Clementine*. "Every hand has its different problems."

The poker game at the back of the saloon is a fixture in every Western, so much so that the voice-over commentary in John Huston's *The Life and Times of Judge Roy Bean* asserts confidently that poker played as great a part in the winning of the West as the Colt revolver or the covered wagon. This may not be strictly accurate but, as I mentioned in chapter 2, poker was the game cowboys played, and it spread west with the frontier. Most of the old-time Hollywood directors were also devoted to the game, and they plotted their films accordingly. So what Andrew Sarris wrote of Bud Boetticher's Westerns applies to the whole genre: they were, he said, "constructed partly as allegorical Odysseys and partly as floating poker games where every character took turns at bluffing about his hand until the final showdown."

As often as not, the showdown involves bluffing a bully or calling his bluff. In *One-Eyed Jacks*, for example, the notorious gunslinger Rio (Marlon Brando) is in jail, waiting to be hanged. His girlfriend smuggles him in a little gambler's pistol. She has the bullets in her hand, but fails to slip them to Brando. Even so, he pulls the empty pistol on the deputy sheriff (Slim Pickens) who is guarding him, demands to be released, and begins to count to ten. Pickens huffs and puffs: the gun's not loaded, he says, and anyway he's out of range. At the count of four, Pickens says, "You're running a bluff, brother, and I'm gonna call you." Brando says, "Go ahead. Try it, Lon," and goes on counting. At the count of eight, Pickens folds: "I'm a-comin'," he says, and unlocks the cell door. The true poker-playing Western hero can even bluff himself out of a death sentence.

There is only one Western, *A Big Hand for the Little Lady*, which is, in itself, all bluff. Henry Fonda, a seemingly reformed poker addict, gets in over his head in a monster game, is dealt—or rather, deals himself—the hand of a lifetime, then collapses of a heart attack before he can play it. His brave little wife, Joanne Woodward, knows nothing about poker but demands to play out his hand—it's all the money they have; the family's future depends on it. So how, she is asked, will she raise the money to bet? She widens her blue eyes and says she will use the cards as collateral for a bank loan. Laughter all round. Everyone at the table knows that the local bank owner abhors gambling. Yet when he sees her cards he opens up the safe, takes out a wad of money, marches her back to the game and orders up chips. The other players fold. It's all a scam, of course: Fonda, Woodward, even their little child are cardsharps, and the banker is in on the plot because he is besotted with the little lady. When, at the end, he has qualms about cheating, their answer is, "We didn't cheat them, we bluffed them. That's the nature of the game." At the poker table, they mean, a scam is just a bluff by any other name, and it

⊗   In this scene from Warner Brothers Pictures' 1966 movie
A Big Hand for the Little Lady, Joanne Woodward showed
that poker wasn't just a man's game.

smells as sweet. It's also a pleasure—the pleasure of outsmarting the smart guys, the storyteller's pleasure of the rattlesnake sting in the tail.

The scam in *A Big Hand for the Little Lady* is all about acting: Woodward, the high-class poker pro, pretends not to know the rules of the game, and Fonda, the card mechanic, fumbles amateurishly with the deck while he deals his opponents killer hands to provoke them into betting. That, too, is poker. Even on a less fanciful, less Hollywood level, the art of bluff usually involves an element of acting. Spanier quotes a classic example of this from James Jones's *From Here to Eternity*: the hero, Prewitt, is playing five-card stud with Warden, his nemesis; on the fourth card, Prew is dealt a third ten (he has one in the hole); Warden, showing a pair of kings, checks, and Prew "raised lightly, very lightly, just a touch, a feeler, a protection bet he could afford to abandon and lose. And Warden, who thought quite a while before he called, looked at his hole card twice and then he almost didn't call, so he had no trips." Warden has his three kings, of course, and breaks poor Prewitt.

In his heart Prew recognizes that Warden is using the bluffer's stock acting ploys to sucker him—the hesitations and feigned reluctance, making as if to bet, then drawing back, knowing all along that he couldn't lose. All that is part of a classic theatrical repertoire—the thousand and one tricks by which one player imposes his will on another, confuses him, bewitches him, leads him on. So when Prew bets out at the end and Warden raises him back, "he made as if to drop out, but he knew he had to call. There was too much of his money in this pot, which was a big one, to chance a bluff."

There is also another style of actor's bluff, the one players call "creating a table image." The grand master of this art is "Crazy Mike" Caro, one of the great theorists of the game and author of books on poker psychology, strategy, and probabilities. He is also a computer expert, the first person to write a program sophisticated enough to give the top players trouble. He earned his nickname by acting the wild man at the table. His technique was to sit down in some gloomy draw poker game in the card rooms at Gardena, stand pat on nothing at all, bet the maximum, and then, when he was called, spread his rubbish cards for all to see, and cackle like a lunatic. The next time he pulled the same stunt, the players would line up to call him and he would have an unbeatable hand. That was back in the late 1960s and Caro added to the confusion by disguising himself as a hippie: straggly beard, long hair, outlandish clothes, strange mannerisms. These days his beard and hair are trimmed, his only eccentricity is a leather fedora, and he has become a world authority. He gives poker seminars, makes poker videos and cassettes, advises software companies, and writes a regular column for *The Card Player* under the byline "America's Mad Genius."

Creating a table image is now a recognized ploy—or it would be if many players were not too arrogant to recognize it. I myself have tried it on twice in America: I exaggerated my English accent, made a big play of my age and my limp and my walking stick, asked the dealer—oh, so politely—to explain the rules of the game to me, called a couple of losing hands cheaply and showed my dreadful cards, and ended up both times winning enough to pay for my vacation.

But it doesn't work in Vegas, where the better players have seen everything, not once but a thousand times. "I can be anywhere in the world," one of the pros told Anthony Holden, when he was writing his book *Big Deal*, "and if I don't know your face, I know I can beat you." Bluffing each other, however, is a tougher proposition, and the skills the top players bring to it have more to do with the imagination than with acting or mathematics or any of the other more pedestrian disciplines which good poker involves.

The subtlest and one of the most famous bluffs of all was run by Jack Straus. I described it in *The Biggest Game in Town*, and since then it has featured in other books as a supreme example of the art of bluffing. This is what happened. In a game of no-limit hold 'em Straus was dealt the worst two cards in the pack, a seven and a deuce of different suits. But he was "on a rush," so he raised anyway, and only one other player stayed with him. The flop was dealt: seven, three, three, giving Straus two pairs—sevens and threes. He bet again, but as he did so he saw his opponent's hand reach quickly for his chips, and Straus knew he had made a mistake. The man, he realized, had a big pair in the hole. He had, in fact, two jacks and, with great confidence, he reraised Straus $5,000. At that point, the logical move was to fold, since Straus was certain he was beaten and that only a bluff could save him. But he called, thereby sowing doubt in the other player's mind. The dealer turned over the fourth card: a deuce. It paired Straus's second hole card but did not improve his hand, since there was already a communal pair of threes on the table. Without hesitating, Straus bet $18,000. There was a long, long silence while the other man considered the implications of the bet. Then Straus leaned forward, smiling his most charming, lopsided smile. "I'll tell you what," he said. "You give me one of those little old $25 chips of yours and you can see either one of my cards, whichever you choose." Another silence. Finally, the man tossed over a green chip and pointed to one of the cards facedown in front of Straus. Straus turned it over: a deuce. Another long silence. The only reasonable explanation for Straus's offer was that the two cards in front of him were paired, so the flop gave him a full house—three deuces to go with the pair of threes on the board. The other man folded his winning hand. When Straus told me about the hand later, he shrugged it off. "It's just a matter of simple psychology," he said.

In poker, as in everything else, imagination starts where logic falters and transforms reality for its own ends, as Straus did with his unplayable cards. His move was more than bluff; it was play in the truest sense—a kind of wit, as playful, stylish, and elegant as any of Oscar Wilde's famous ripostes. And play, after all, is where poker started and what, in the end, it is all about.

CHAPTER 6

FAMOUS HANDS
and
BAD BEATS

Mischa Auer: "I've met every king in Europe."

Marlene Dietrich: "Now you've met two aces in Bottleneck!"

Destry Rides Again

⊗ opposite page: Marlene Dietrich and Mischa Auer in a scene
from Universal Pictures' 1939 film *Destry Rides Again*.

"THE GOOD NEWS IS THAT IN EVERY DECK OF FIFTY-TWO CARDS there are 2,598,960 possible five-card poker hands," Anthony Holden wrote in *Big Deal.* "The bad news is that you are only going to be dealt one of them." Most of the time, that one hand is going to be worthless.

When you look at your hole cards in a game of hold 'em—always with the same little stir of excitement and anticipation—the odds against finding a pair of aces looking back at you are 220 to one, 72.7 to one against a high pair (two kings through two jacks), and the overall odds against seeing any pair at all are sixteen to one—roughly once, that is, in every two rounds of play. Every so often, however, you strike gold. Once in a game of pot-limit hold 'em, for example—just once in more than forty years of poker playing—I made a royal straight flush of hearts on Fourth Street. The odds against that happening were 19,599 to one, but that's not why I remember the hand. I remember it because it looked so pretty and won me so little. My opponent had two aces in his hand, and there was an ace and two hearts on the flop, but when a third heart was dealt on Fourth Street he was too canny—or timid—to call even the small amount I bet.

It isn't always like that. On one famous occasion, a contestant in "the big one," the $10,000 no-limit hold 'em tournament in the World Series, was dealt two black aces in his very first hand. A pair of aces is the most powerful of all starting hands in hold 'em, so he raised strongly and got one caller. The dealer

dealt out the flop—ace of hearts, king of hearts, king of spades, giving the raiser a full house, aces over kings. He bet modestly, $2,000, a come-on bet to draw the other man in. To his delight, his opponent reraised another $2,000. This was what he had been hoping for. "Raise," he said. He put his hands behind the stacks of chips in front of him, and moved them all into the pot. The other man looked at him carefully, looked at the mass of chips in the middle of the table, studied his cards. Finally, he shrugged and pushed the rest of his chips forward. Since all the money was in the center and there could be no more betting, the two players turned over their hole cards, as etiquette required. The man with the full house was afraid the other player would show a pair of kings, making him four of a kind; the least he expected to see was an ace and a king. Instead, when his opponent saw the pair of aces, he shook his head despondently and turned over a queen and a jack of hearts. He had four to a royal straight flush, but there was only one card in the deck that could win for him. In the first hand of the World Championship, with the best poker players on earth all around, he had bet everything on a forty-four-to-one shot. He rose from his chair, ready to make a humiliated exit. The dealer paused dramatically,

- FAINT - HEART - NEVER -
- FILLED - A - SPADE - FLUSH -

⊗ A 1905 illustration.

thumped the table, and dealt the ten of hearts. Five minutes after the tournament started, the man with aces full was out, $10,000 poorer.

These are the kinds of hands that poker players talk about when they get together. They don't talk about the hands they have won. They talk, instead, about "bad beats," the hands they should have won but didn't, because the cards were freakish or, more often, because some other player made a stupid call.

Bad-beat stories are long-winded and ill-tempered, they never have a happy ending, and their punch line is always roughly the same: "I mean, what was the schmuck doing in the hand anyway with a pair of lousy deuces?" Bad beats go against all the principles on which good poker is based: logic, calculation, percentages, and the immutable laws of probability. They are as irrational as dreams, and they haunt you like nightmares. You brood about them, you complain about them, you play them over in your head again and again. And this is how it should be, because while it is happening a truly bad beat feels like a waking nightmare.

I still vividly remember my own worst nightmare and bad beat, even though it happened a dozen or more years ago. It was in the final of a big pot-limit hold 'em tournament in London, the field had been narrowed to two, and I was head-to-head with Mickey Finn, an amiable American professional player who makes his living on the European circuit. I was dealt a pair of kings in the hole—the best hand I had seen all night—and when Mickey, who was on the small blind, bet into me I raised the pot. He called. The flop was king, eight, six, of different suits. I trap-checked my three kings, and he came out betting, just as I had hoped. When I called his bet and moved all in, Mickey, who had twice as many chips as I, called without hesitation. I turned over my pair of kings; he turned over a five and seven, off-suit. The eight and six in the flop gave him an open-ended straight, and he didn't even have to wait to fill it: the next card the dealer flipped out was a four. I still had chances: ten of the forty-five cards left in the deck—three eights, three sixes, three fours, and the case king—would give me a full house or quads; all the dealer had to do was pair one of the cards on Fifth Street. But he dealt a useless jack, Mickey Finn took the £5,000 first prize, and I had to settle for £2,500 and a long-running recurrent nightmare. Afterward, when I asked Mickey why he had raised before the flop with such dreadful cards and then called my initial reraise, he said, "It was a semibluff. I was putting one of those Vegas moves on you." So maybe it wasn't a bad beat, after all. Maybe I was simply outmaneuvered by a player who is far subtler than I will ever be. But I still can't get over the injustice of it.

Famous hands are not always bad beats, although the most famous of them all might be interpreted that way—two aces and two eights, the cards Wild Bill Hickok was holding on August 2, 1876, in Nuttall and Mann's saloon in Deadwood, South Dakota. He won the pot but was shot in the back of the head by Crooked Nose McCall before he could enjoy it. Since then, aces and eights have not been popular with

⊗ *Wild Bill Hickok at the Cards,* painted by N. C. Wyeth in 1916.

poker players. They are called "dead man's hand."

There are other poker hands unusual enough to have names, though none are so dramatic. Ten-deuce, for example, is known as a "Doyle Brunson." They are a virtually unplayable hold 'em hand, yet Brunson won the World Championship with them two years in a row because, in the final stages of the tournament, the antes are so high that he had to call the initial blind bet, regardless of the cards in his hand, his opponent didn't raise, and the flop gave Brunson a full house.

Most of the other named hands—there are dozens of them—are merely nicknames. Here are a few:

American Airlines: AA; two aces
The Alabama Night Riders: K-K-K; three kings
Broderick Crawford: 10-4; ten four
Baskin Robbins: 3-Ace; thirty-one
Big Slick: A-K

"DRAW POKER"
(RAISING HIM THE "LIMIT.")

Woolworth: 5-10; five and dime
Oldsmobile: 9-8; ninety-eight
The Gay Waiters: Q-Q-3-3; queens and treys
A Pair of Dogs: K-9, K-9; two K-9s
Jesse James: 4-5; forty-five
The Royal Couples: K-K-Q-Q; kings and queens
The Musical Group or Motown: J-J-5-5; jacks 'n fives
Hughie, Dewie, and Lewie: 2-2-2; three deuces
Hunting Season: A-A-2-2; bullets and ducks

None of these nicknames would win prizes at a festival of wit, but in the average poker game, where hours of subtle play and maneuvering can pass without anyone saying anything except "check," "raise," and "fold," at least they break the monotony.

Famous hands are famous and bad beats hurt

"THREE LITTLE QUEENS"
(A DAISY HAND!)

⊗ left: *Three Little Queens*, originally used in the 1887 book *Poker* by J. Prescott Schenck, was later featured on several trading cards.

⊗ top: *Draw Poker* is another *Poker* illustration that would appear in decks.

because both illustrate the one simple rule that is the foundation of all good play: *you win at poker by not losing*. This truism is not quite as blindingly obvious as it first seems. Instead, it is another way of expressing an equally hallowed truth: the best players are those who win most with their good hands and lose least with the less good. Winning, that is, sometimes means throwing away apparently powerful cards, the kind most players fall so much in love with that they can't let them go.

Here is an example of the art of folding at the highest level. In one of those insanely high-stakes games of no-limit hold 'em that rarely take place anywhere except in Las Vegas—the buy-in was $100,000—Doyle Brunson looked at his hole cards and found a pair of aces. He bet strongly and was called by two players, A and B. The flop was ace, deuce, four, all of different suits, giving Brunson trip aces. Again he bet heavily—$25,000—and again both the other players called. Fourth Street was a second deuce, so the board now looked like this: A-2-4-2. With his pair of aces in the hole, Brunson now had the strongest possible full house, aces over deuces. Nevertheless, he checked to see what would happen. Player A came out betting, and player B moved all in with a massive raise. Brunson thought for a long time, then folded his top full house. Player A called. The dealer dealt the last card, a second four, making: A-2-4-2-4. Both players had four of a kind: A had quad fours; B had quad deuces.

These things happen, of course, despite the odds. Once in every hundred-or-so thousand hands, two players will both be dealt quads, and one of them is going to lose a lot of money. Brunson's genius was to fold aces-full, a hand the rest of us would usually kill for.

Looking at it coldly, later, it seems a reasonable enough thing to have done. When Brunson bet big before the flop, A and B would have read him for a high pair in the hole—most probably two aces, two kings, or, at worst, ace-king suited. So they would have had to have pairs in their hands to call him. And when he bet again strongly after the flop what else could either of them have called him with except trips? (The only hand that could have beaten him at that point was a straight—the flop was A, 2, 4—but the game was too hard and too expensive for anyone to have called his big preflop bet with a worthless three and five.) So when the board paired, Brunson knew one of them must have made quads. Even so, it took exceptionally iron discipline and cold-eyed calculation to fold his massive hand. After all, there was still one more ace in the deck to make him unbeatable. But he didn't like the odds. He contributed $30,000 to the pot, but it would have cost him $100,000 if he'd stayed to the end. Player A won the pot, but only because he defied the odds and got lucky. Compared to Brunson, he played his hand badly.

This extraordinary hand illustrates another immortal poker truth: no one, say the professionals, ever bluffs a made hand. What they mean is that if you bet with very strong cards and someone who isn't a fool raises, then he is holding the miracle hand that can beat you. That is why Brunson folded his full house of aces, and it is what Amarillo Slim Preston meant when he said, "If you can't fold the winning hand, you can't play poker." One legendary gambler liked his cards so much that he bet his glass eye on them, and when he was raised he offered to tear out his good eye to reraise the raiser. If something like that ever happens to you, do not call. One sharp eye is enough to read the cards. The guy's got his immortal hand, however improbable it may be.

"No one ever bluffs a made hand" is the simple truth that undermines one of the most discussed, and least satisfactory, of all fictional poker hands, the showdown in *The Cincinnati Kid* between Lancey Howard, a.k.a. "the Man" (Edward G. Robinson),

⊗ opposite page: Doyle Brunson studies the situation.

and "the Kid" (Steve McQueen). David Spanier and Anthony Holden devote pages of their books to it, and Michael Weisenberg analyzed it in great statistical detail in his column in the magazine *Card Player*. Both Richard Jessup's novel and Norman Jewison's movie version are full of good things, much appreciated by poker players, especially Lancey's classic answer to the question, Did he really have a pair?: "All you pay is the looking price. Lessons are extra." Authentic poker only goes out of the window at the final showdown when, in a game of five-card stud, the Kid's full house is beaten by the Man's straight flush. Weisenberg, who is a mathematician, worked out the improbable chances of that ever happening. This is how Holden summarized his findings:

The odds against any full house being beaten by *any* straight flush, in a two-handed game, are 45,102,784:1; the odds against these two particular hands coinciding are stratospheric. Given that the Kid's full house contains tens, and that one ten is already in his opponent's hand, the chances that *both* these hands will appear in one deal of two-handed five-card stud have been calculated at a laughable 332,220,508,619:1—or well over three *billion:*1 against. If these two played fifty hands of stud an hour, eight hours a day, five days a week, the situation should arise about once every 443 years.

In a situation like that, Weisenberg concludes, any experienced poker player would assume that he had been set up, that the deck was fixed, and that Lancey and the dealer were in cahoots. Instead, he docilely bows his head and accepts his status as a second-class citizen in the poker world.

Improbabilities aside, the Kid's humiliation is partly deserved. Spanier points out that he makes two highly unprofessional mistakes. The first is on card

four of the deal when the Kid, who has the queen of hearts in the hole and is showing two tens, catches a second queen; Lancey is showing the seven, eight, and ten of hearts. There is almost $6,000 in the pot, but instead of betting it all, the Kid bets a mere $1,000, offering, as Spanier says, seven-to-one odds on a three-to-one chance of making his flush. On the last card, the Kid draws a third queen, and Lancey draws the magic nine of hearts. This is where the Kid makes his second mistake: sure, he has his full house—queens over tens—but he is looking at a possible straight flush. If the Kid had been the great player he's cracked up to be, he'd have checked, knowing that the Man would be too canny to bet a mere flush into a possible full house. Instead, he comes out betting like any amateur bewitched by his cards. Worse still, when Lancey raises him back, he calls. Didn't anybody tell him that no one ever bluffs with a made hand?

Or don't they? It would have been a masterly showdown if Lancey had been bluffing all along. He would truly have been the Man if he had had a useless card in the hole but, as Holden writes in *Big Deal*, he "intimidated the Kid into folding his full house, then rubbed salt in the wound by revealing a much inferior hand. This is how noble spirits can be broken at the poker table. And this is the real purpose of the game: to use whatever cards are on display to bend other wills to your own. No poker player ever earned any respect simply by pulling good cards; the best players are those who can turn indifferent hands into winners through psychological mastery of their opponents." That is how Nixon played his cards during the Watergate scandal. But he wasn't playing against a top professional, or for the benefit of the untutored audience of a movie or a novel. For their sake, the confrontation in *The Cincinnati Kid* is turned into a poker version of *Jurassic Park*—a

⊗ Steve McQueen in a poker showdown in
MGM's 1965 movie *The Cincinnati Kid*.

giant hand against a monster, a brontosaurus versus Tyrannosaurus rex. From the aficionado's point of view, a game of great subtlety is reduced to blind chance and parody. Lancey won by blind luck, not by superior skill; he drew a miracle card, and the Kid suffered the ultimate bad beat.

Some games are famous simply because of the amount of money at stake. The three-time World Champion Johnny Moss once told me about a game of seven-card stud in which everyone anted $800 a hand, the dealer bet $1,600 blind (without looking at his hole cards), the low card brought it in (that is, was forced to bet) for $3,200, and the opening raise was $6,400. "I won eight hunnerd and seventy thousand dollars that night—the most I ever did make in one game," Moss said. "The biggest check"—chip—"they had was a hunnerd-dollar black. I had racks of them piled up on the floor beside my chair; there warn't no room on the table." I asked him who had been playing. "Coast gamblers, guys from Los Angeles," he answered, then added helpfully, "rich people, mostly." Eric Drache was more forthcoming: "I suspect not too much tax had been paid on that money," he said. "It wasn't a poker game; it was a laundromat."

Even those numbers seem small compared to the biggest single pot of five-card stud ever recorded—the $797,000 won by Arnold Rothstein when his diamond flush beat Nick the Greek Dandolas's pair of kings. This was during the early 1920s, when Rothstein and Nick the Greek were the most famous gamblers in America. Rothstein, the only person ever to have fixed the baseball World Series (in 1919), won $500,000 on the first Dempsey-Tunney fight and another $800,000 on a colt called Sidereal, at Aqueduct, in 1921. He was a man with many nicknames: the police called him "the J. P. Morgan of the Underworld"; the underworld called him "the Big Bankroll"

or "the Man Uptown"; Damon Runyon called him "the Brain"; and Scott Fitzgerald turned him into Wolfsheim, the gambler in *The Great Gatsby*. Rothstein was eventually murdered on November 4, 1928, for nonpayment of a gambling debt—$475,000 that he dropped in a poker game he claimed was fixed.

Nick the Greek's gambling was equally outrageous. He claimed to have won and lost hundreds of millions of dollars during his lifetime. When he arrived in Las Vegas in 1949, the Greek was fifty-seven years old—a tall, trim man, soft-spoken and elegantly dressed, with a degree from an English university. He was known as "the king of gamblers" and was reputed to have broken all the high rollers back East, including the late and now legendary Arnold Rothstein. He was looking, he said, for a high-stakes poker game, but all he could find in Vegas were ring games, with seven or eight players and limits on the betting. The Greek wanted to play no-limit poker, heads-up with a single opponent. So he went to see Benny Binion. Binion had been boss of gambling in Dallas but had to leave town precipitately in 1946 when, as he put it, "my sheriff got beat in the election." He moved to Las Vegas, where gambling was legal, and eventually bought the Horseshoe, a shabby little casino that had begun life in 1937 as the El Dorado Club. Binion, with a shrewd eye for free publicity for his newly acquired casino, offered to set up a game, provided it was played in public. When the Greek agreed, Binion called his friend Johnny Moss, in Dallas. Moss got in his car, drove to Vegas, shook hands with the Greek, and sat down immediately to play.

In the weeks that followed, the Greek got his action and Binion got his publicity, to a degree that neither of them could have imagined. The game lasted for five months, with breaks for sleep every four or five days, although the Greek, who was fifteen

⊗ Las Vegas casino owner Benny Binion is seen here with
"king of gamblers" Nick the Greek in the early 1950s.

years older than Moss, spent most of his nonpoker time at the craps tables and needled Moss about his frailty, saying, "What are you going to do, Johnny—sleep your life away?" But even before the first break, the table, which Benny had thoughtfully positioned near the entrance to the casino, was surrounded by crowds six deep, drawn by rumors of the biggest game the town had ever seen.

They began by playing five-card stud—"not my real strong game," Moss said—and during the weeks of this, while occasional players came and went, buying themselves into the game with a minimum stake of $10,000, Moss and the Greek played what has since become one of the most famous and expensive hands in the history of poker.

In the game as Moss and the Greek were playing

it, each anted $100, and the man with the lowest exposed card "brought it in" for $200. Before this particular deal started, each had about a quarter of a million dollars' worth of chips in front of him; by the time it was over, the entire half-million was in the pot.

Moss's first two cards were a nine in the hole and a six exposed; the Greek was showing a seven. Moss told me the story back in 1981, as he had told it often before, with a kind of chewed-up relish. His Texas drawl was so thick and slurred that it sounded at times like a foreign language, but the sentences were as economical as telegrams: "Low man brings it in. I bet two hunnerd with a six, he raises fifteen hunnerd or two thousand, I call him. The next card comes, I catch a nine, he catches a six. I got two nines then. I make a good bet—five thousand, maybe—an' he plays back at me, twenty-five thousand. I jus' call him. I'm figurin' to take all that money of his, an' I don't wanna scare him none. The next card comes, he catches a trey, I catch a deuce. Ain't nuttin' he got can beat my two nines. I check then to trap him, an' he bets, jus' like I wanted. So I raise him wa-ay up there, an' he calls. I got him in there, all right. There's a hunnerd thousand dollars in that pot—maybe more; I don't know exactly—an' I'm a-winnin' it. On the end, I catch a trey, he catches a jack. He's high now with the jack an' he bets fifty thousand. I cain't put him on no jack in the hole, you know. He ain't gonna pay all that money jus' for the chance to outdraw me. I don't care what he catches, he's gotta beat those two nines of mine. So I move in with the rest of my money."

In the moments of silence after Moss pushed what remained of his quarter of a million dollars' worth of chips into the center, the Greek eyed him, upright and unblinking, and then said softly, "Mr. Moss, I think I have a jack in the hole."

"Greek," Moss replied, "if you got a jack down there, you're liable to win yourself one helluva pot."

There was another aching silence, and then the Greek carefully pushed his own chips forward and turned over his hole card. It was the jack of diamonds.

"He outdrew me," Moss said. "We had about two hunnerd an' fifty thousand dollars apiece in that pot, and he win it. But that was all right. I broke him anyway."

That was the old man talking, secure in his fame, his three world titles, and his investments, and as remorseless as he had always been, the kind of character that John Wayne was fond of portraying—true grit without forgiveness, to be admired, but only from a safe distance.

In the course of their marathon, Moss and Nick the Greek played most forms of poker. They switched from five-card stud to draw, seven-card stud, seven-card hi-lo split, and both forms of low ball—ace-to-the-five and deuce-to-the-seven—and, gradually, Moss wore his opponent down. After almost exactly five months, the Greek lost his last pot, smiled courteously, and said in his soft voice, "Mr. Moss, I have to let you go." He bowed slightly and went upstairs to bed. Precisely how much he had lost is not certain; the rumor says two million.

When Johnny Moss and Nick the Greek played their legendary game, Moss was a smooth-cheeked man, forty-two years old, with thinning hair, wide-set eyes, and a thin, scrolled mouth. By the time he told me about it he was seventy-five and he looked like a basilisk: his eyes were hooded and bleak, his face was like saddle leather, there were deep lines carved from his nose almost to his chin, and his rather elegantly shaped mouth was retracted in permanent distaste. But he was still playing in the big games and winning tournaments. And he went on playing in the $20–$40 hold 'em game at the Horseshoe right up until he died, in December 1995, at the age of eighty-eight.

Nick the Greek was less fortunate. In his prime, when he was winning and losing hundreds of thousands of dollars, he liked to say, in his elegant, educated way, "The exhilaration of this form of economic existence is beyond my power to describe." But the losses got to him in the end, and he finished up playing $5–$10–limit draw in Gardena. When a fellow player asked him, cruelly, if this wasn't a comedown from his glory days, the Greek replied, "It's action, isn't it?" He died broke on Christmas Day in 1966.

⊗ Johnny Moss is joined by Jack Binion on Johnny's 86th birthday.

CHAPTER 7

THE WORLD SERIES,
1994

The next best thing to gambling and winning is gambling and losing.

Nick the Greek

⊗ opposite page: The exterior of Benny Binion's Horseshoe
Casino, circa 1958. The Horseshoe hosts the annual World
Series of Poker.

THE WORLD SERIES OF POKER, which takes place annually at Binion's Horseshoe in Las Vegas, and runs from late April to mid-May, is the most popular, the most prestigious, and the longest running of all poker tournaments. It began in 1970, when Benny Binion invited a handful of his poker-playing cronies—some were professionals and some were amateurs, but all of them were high rollers and most were Texans—to get together at the Horseshoe to compete against one another in various forms of poker at stakes only they could contemplate.

When all the games were over, they voted democratically for who should be nominated the champion of champions. The man they elected, by unanimous decision, was Johnny Moss. How much money Moss won during that first unofficial tournament is not recorded, but the Binions commemorated his victory by giving him a massive silver cup with his name engraved on it.

Since that first tournament, the event has grown exponentially. By 1990, the entry to the main event—the $10,000 no-limit Texas hold 'em World Championship—was approaching the magic number of two hundred. Two hundred buy-ins meant $2,000,000 to be distributed in prize money— about 40 percent to the winner, the rest according to finishing place. The Binions, who understand what makes gamblers tick, stopped fussing with percentages and guaranteed the world champion $1,000,000, as well as the fourteen-karat-gold bracelet with his or her name on it that is also given to the winner of each of the subsidiary events. For the Silver Anniversary in 1994, Jack Binion, who has been president of the Horseshoe since 1964, added a further attraction: the champion would win his weight in silver as well as $1,000,000 and anyone who made it into the money in the minor events would receive a commemorative silver bar.

Like the World Series, the Horseshoe Casino itself has grown enormously in recent years. When I first went there, in 1981, it was a shabby little place, dark and narrow, and in terms of decor it had nothing to offer at all. It was also overpoweringly noisy, for the simple reason that it was always packed. If you wanted action—real action with no upper limits on the bets you made—forget the ritzy palaces on the strip; the Horseshoe was the place to go. It wasn't glamorous; there were no Roman slave girls to serve you drinks or trapeze artists swinging around above your head while you gambled, no pricey shops, no tennis courts, no golf courses. At the Horseshoe, what you saw was what you got: gambling without frills but also without limits.

Somehow, the Binions had worked out the right formula for serious gamblers. Although Benny Binion had left Dallas in a hurry, his connections guaranteed him the loyalty of the high-rolling Texans. Supporting Benny was the patriotic thing to do, and anyway, the Binions were their sort of folk. The Binions responded by providing their sort of outsized gambling action, along with the best steaks and the hottest chili in town. Yet even the most loyal Texans drew the line at staying in the handful of pokey rooms above the casino. They gambled at the Horseshoe but stayed across the road at the Golden Nugget, particularly after Steve Wynne refurbished the hotel from top to bottom, put in a huge pool, and made it as luxurious as any palace on the strip.

The Binions eventually solved the accommodation problem by buying the casino next door, a great, echoing barn of a place called the Mint, which was nearly always deserted and had just two things to recommend it, both of them on its roof: a small swimming pool—the only one downtown in the early 1980s—and a huge illuminated clock (also the only one downtown, then and now, in a city where time has been officially banished in case it interferes with business). The Mint had a lot of rooms, none of them particularly luxurious, but considerably more comfortable than the flophouse above the Horseshoe. The Binions did almost nothing to tart up the place or improve the amenities. They simply knocked down the wall between the two casinos, removed the giant illuminated "M" from the clock, put a horseshoe in its place, and called the whole block Binion's Horseshoe. And that was all it took. Overnight, the wastelands of the Mint were jam-packed with gamblers whooping it up and having a great time.

During the World Series, the crowds reach saturation point as hundreds of poker players fly in from all over the world. Most are amateurs, and they come from every corner of the United States, from Great Britain, Ireland, Germany, France, and Italy, from Scandinavia, Australia, Costa Rica. In 1994, there was even a twenty-one-strong deputation from New Caledonia, a tiny group of islands in the South Pacific; they spoke French, and most of them seemed to know only four words of English: *bet, check, raise,* and *fold.* The players come in all shapes and sizes, although the predominant size is extra-large. (When one 350-pounder left the table I was playing at, a wag called out, "Two seats here, floorman.") The out-of-towners are there primarily to compete in the tournaments, which cover most current forms of poker and vary in expense from the thousand-dollar-buy-in women's seven-card stud to the ten-thousand-dollar-buy-in World Championship. The Las Vegas professionals play in the tournaments, too, but often simply as a courtesy to Jack Binion and because their status as champions requires it. Their real business is in the side games that go on day and night, nonstop, while the World Series is in progress.

These cash games are listed in a kind of short-hand on a roster at the back of the tournament area. The smallest is "PLH 1-2-5"—pot-limit hold 'em, in which the compulsory blind bets are $1, $2, and $5, and the buy-in is $500; from there, the size of the games climbs steadily toward the stratosphere. The biggest game of all is off in a corner on table 61, where ex-champions like Doyle Brunson, Johnny Chan, and Stu Ungar hold court. According to the

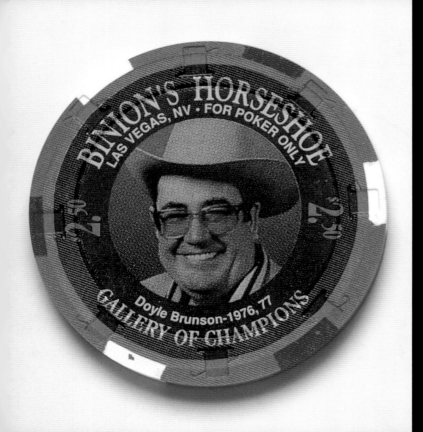

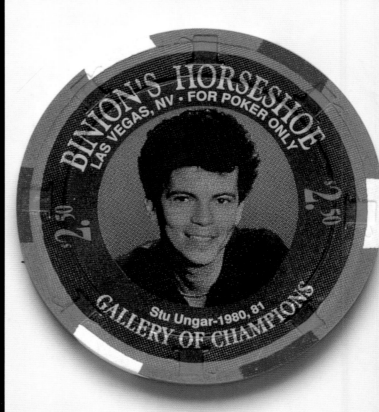

⊗ Silver Anniversary of the Poker World Series chip dedicated
to Doyle Brunson.

⊗ Silver Anniversary of the Poker World Series chip dedicated
to Stu Ungar.

⊗ Silver Anniversary of the Poker World Series chip dedicated to Johnny Moss.

⊗ Silver Anniversary of the Poker World Series chip dedicated to "Amarillo Slim" Preston.

board, the game on table 61 is "2/7 NL, 100 ante, 200–400"—that is, deuce-to-the-seven razz, a particularly savage form of low ball in which each player antes $100 dollars before every hand, the two players to the left of the dealer are forced to bet $200 and $400 blind, and there is no limit to the size of the subsequent bets. The buy-in for that game is $25,000, although no one usually sits down with so little. One night during my stay, someone at the table won a single pot of nearly $100,000. In other words, the World Series is not just the foremost poker tournament; it is also a hustlers' convention, a brief season, like the run-up to Christmas on Fifth Avenue,

when the professionals reckon to make enough money to set themselves up for the year ahead.

The first time I watched the World Series, in 1981, I was bug-eyed with wonder, like a visitor from Mars. And indeed, there was a great deal to wonder at, starting with the giant sums of money involved. Back then, there were no cheap ways of entering a tournament, and the players in the World Championship event were truly the elect, the highest of high-rolling amateurs—oil men, movie moguls, investment bankers, rich doctors and lawyers, a few gangsters, and a handful of tough and classy women—to whom ten grand meant more or less nothing and who were

⊗ The winners of the first Women's Seven Card Stud Tournaments, 1976–1981, pose for a group shot.

playing purely for the pleasure of sitting down with the best poker players in the world. As for the top professionals, money was not their problem; if they were temporarily short there were always big-time gamblers to stake them in return for a slice of their winnings.

Over the years, the World Series acquired a great deal of glamour in the poker world and inspired a large number of imitations. But one major problem remained: how to attract all those good players who were out there yearning to get in but who were never going to build up enough money for a stake. In 1984, someone had the smart idea of organizing "satellites"—competitions for the competitions—in which ten players would ante up $1,000 each and play a freeze-out, winner take all. But even $1,000 is a substantial sum to invest in a nine-to-one shot, and it was still beyond the range of many hopefuls. The next step was super satellites—multitable events in which each player paid $220 for two hundred chips and, during the first hour, could rebuy additional stacks of two hundred for $200 a throw. If enough people entered—and they entered by the hundreds—there would be sufficient money to guarantee everyone at the final table an entry to the main event. There are now satellites for all the events. At the Horseshoe, they start a few days before the beginning of the World Series, but for months before that they had been running in casinos across America and around the world. The World Series is no longer the exclusive preserve of the top professionals and the millionaires; it has been democratized.

Like all poker players, I had dreamed of playing in the World Championship. In 1994, I finally got my chance. I had been training for it for fifteen months, playing in tournaments once or twice a week in London. Although I often reached the final table and occasionally won an event, I knew that in Vegas

they marched to a different tune. I would be like a good club tennis player with a wild-card entry to Wimbledon: the game played by the top players has no relation to the game played by the likes of me; it just looks the same. But at least I could try not to make a fool of myself. I would pace myself, get used to the pressures, work out some strategies for survival.

The basic strategy was to stay sane in an insane environment, which meant getting in shape both mentally and physically. The physical part was straightforward: first, get over the jet lag (I arrived almost two weeks before the main event), then establish a routine in which poker was only one part: regular meals, plenty of sleep, and twenty laps of the pool each morning before breakfast. The mental training was harder. The first step was to create an orderly space within the ambient lunacy, a space that contained books to read, a computer to work on, and television news to remind myself that there was a world elsewhere.

A key part of that private space was the little balcony outside the picture windows of my room. From up there on the twenty-second floor of the Horseshoe, the view was spectacular: out across the railroad tracks and the ring road to the blue mountains circling the horizon, down onto the crowds on Fremont Street and the maze of pipes, steel walkways, and air ducts on the casino roofs. At night, the mountains disappeared, and the town became a blaze of lights: rivers of colored neon cascading down the fronts of the buildings and reflecting in the opaque glass of the Golden Nugget's tower block, a sea of smaller lights stretching out across the desert, and, up above, the winking lights of hovering choppers and the planes coming and going from the airport. Even from high up, it was never quiet out on the balcony; the air-conditioning plants kept up a steady roar, and every few minutes the giant cowboy above the entrance of the Pioneer Club down on Fremont saluted the passersby and repeated, in a tinny voice, "Howdy, pardner. Welcome to Las Vegas." (Benny Binion cheered when Amarillo Slim blasted the cowboy with a shotgun from his window in the Horseshoe because the voice kept him awake.) Despite the noise, room 2208 was a fine and private place to retreat to, and I spent a good deal of time there. Then, when I was good and ready, I would go downstairs and play cards.

Poker is a game of many skills, but there is one, not often mentioned, that separates the professionals from the amateurs: somewhere along the road, the pros have lost their sense of urgency. For them, their lives are one long poker game, which began when they turned professional and will end—if it ever ends—when they retire to the Great Poker Game in the Sky. Mostly they reckon to win, but sometimes they lose, and when they do they shrug and leave the table and come back the next day or the next week, knowing the game will always be there. Amateurs are less philosophical: because they usually play no more than once or twice a week, they want to cram as much action as they can into the limited time at their disposal. So they stay too long at the table and play until they can't think straight.

To survive in Vegas, you must divest yourself of that sense of urgency. Day or night, the game you want is always in progress, and you must treat it as the professionals do: when nothing is going right, when you sit for hours folding unplayable hands, or, worse, when every time you are dealt two kings someone else has a pair of aces, you must learn to get up from the table, swallow your losses, and come back another time. Quitting when you are ahead is easy; to cut your losses and run takes far greater discipline.

One morning I had breakfast with Mickey Finn, my worst-beat nemesis from London. Finn is an affable man, but that morning he looked grim. "I'm running bad," he said. "I've dropped ten big ones since I arrived." "Now what?" I asked. His face brightened. "I've drawn a line under it and I'm starting over," he said. "I feel much better."

Finn has played a lot of cards in Vegas, and he understands the pressures. Many of the British contingent were newcomers to the scene who got off the plane, took a taxi to Binion's, and were promptly swallowed alive. Normally, the poker room at the Horseshoe is buried away in a far corner of the casino, but during the World Series a large area in front of the reception desk is cleared of slot machines and becomes the tournament poker pit. As a result, you are already engulfed in the action even before you

⊗ Cover of a deck from Russell Playing Cards of New York, dating from the 1920s or 1930s.

have checked in. Right behind you is a sea of intent faces; the dealers are deftly flicking out the cards, summoning cocktail waitresses, announcing vacant seats; the voices on the intercom summon players to the telephone; and faintly, beneath it all, is a rattling sound, like surf on shingle, as the players riffle their stacks of chips up and down and in and out, waiting for a playable hand. All this is music to the poker addict's ear, the sweet music of action, and for some of the London mob it was irresistible. They arrived with cheap flight tickets they couldn't change, went straight to the tables without bothering to unpack their bags, got caught up in the fever, and blew all their money. Forty-eight hours later, they were huddled together, penniless, up on the pool deck, waiting for their flights home and too broke to eat even at Binion's coffee shop, which is famous for its $4 steak dinners. "Be a pal," they would mutter. "Nick us a couple of bananas from the buffet." But at least the sunshine was free, and they went home with great tans.

Others, less innocent, had come with bigger bank rolls, prepared for battle, and had then been destroyed. Fat Felix, for example, is a steady winner in the big games at the London casinos. At the Horseshoe, he was wandering around dazed, like a man who has been mugged. He had been in town for three weeks, he told me, and had dropped $60,000. When I commiserated with him, his Arab melancholy overflowed. He squeezed my hand gratefully, then ambled off, shaking his head. When I saw him again a couple of days later, he had lost another $10,000. But later, back in London, all he said was, "It was worth it. I had a wonderful time."

Fat Felix was not necessarily playing badly; he had simply been mesmerized by the flood tide of money that washes around the place during the World Series. The illusion that money means nothing is fed spectacularly by the professional poker players. They walk around in cheap nylon bomber jackets and soiled T-shirts. If you saw them on the street you would give them a buck. Then they fish about in the pockets of their tattered jeans and pull out inch-thick wads of $100 bills, held together by rubber bands. All of it is legal tender, but none of it is for buying things. Money to the professionals is merely a tool, an instrument they need to ply their trade. It has no reality for them, except in the intricate calculations of a poker game, and that is a reality they understand down to the last tiny nuance. All the amateurs can see, however, are huge sums that seem to be casually up for grabs. The sight bewitches them, and they blow off their own resources scrambling for the illusory pot of gold.

For four weeks each year, Binion's is the craziest place on earth, and it takes enormous self-control simply to stay sane. Yet the atmosphere is curiously festive, and disdain for money is part of the festivity. In the little $1-$2-$5 pot-limit game, the first player to act says, "A quarter to go" and throws in a green $25 chip. An elderly man wearing a white Stetson and a white cavalry shirt flicks a $100 bill into the pot and says, "Make it a dollar straight." The dealer thumps the table and deals three spades into the center. Without hesitating, the man who had originally bet the "quarter" now bets $250. The man in the white Stetson looks at him, looks at the exposed cards, shrugs, and throws his cards faceup into the center: an ace and king of hearts. "Right string, wrong yo-yo," he barks. But the very next deal he comes out raising again before the flop. "Don't mess with him," another player says as he folds his hand. "He's hotter than a polar bear in the Mojave Desert." Three players call, however, then fold docilely when white Stetson bets $500 after the flop. "It's like picking fresh grapes," someone says admiringly. "The bigger they are, the easier it is." White Stetson beams.

Large sums are changing hands, yet the poker tables buzz with the pleasure and excitement and good humor that come when people get together to do something they love doing and do well. When someone wins a hand because another player checked when he should have bet, the winner scoops in the chips and says, wonderingly, "Only in America can a guy get a free card and make money. Only in America."

Another element of the festivity is the food. All day and every day, Jack Binion lays on a lavish banquet for the players, starting with the mother of all breakfasts: all the juices, all the fruits, and every hot dish you ever dreamed of and were afraid to ask for all at once. There is a chef to cook your eggs just so, another chef to carve your ham, another hovering in case of emergency, and teams of white-jacketed waiters to top up the hot plates of hash, sausage, bacon, pork chops, and French toast. Dinner is on the same scale: mountains of oysters and crab legs and shrimp, great roasts of beef and turkey, giant bowls of salad, rows of hotplates full of chops, chicken legs, fish, and vegetables, and racks of rich desserts. The abundance contributes to the unreality. I saw a man piling blackberries and raspberries onto a plateful of beef and potatoes, a willowy old lady who took five chocolate eclairs, paused, considered, then took a sixth. It is all part of the holiday atmosphere; in food, as in poker, anything goes.

The revels end abruptly when you sit down to play a tournament. In 1994, there were twenty-one open events in the World Series, and each of them was like the last-chance saloon: the atmosphere was gloomy, the faces were tense and unsmiling, and, as P. G. Wodehouse put it, "the general chit-chat was pretty well down-and-out." The reason is simple: if you make a mistake or suffer a bad beat in a cash game, you can always reach into your pocket and pull out more money, but if you make a mistake in a tournament you are out.

For players like me, there is another cause for alarm, and it has to do with pride. The tournament events are our chance to sit down with the champions on equal terms—or rather, on equal financial terms at the start. "We're ambitious amateurs, and we don't want to be humiliated," said my friend Julian Studley, a New Yorker who plays regularly and successfully in the big tournaments. "The great players don't have that problem. They'll go for the brilliant, do-or-die move, and if it doesn't come off and they get eliminated, so what? It doesn't bother them. We are different. We want to stick around because our egos are very much affected by being able to say we were still there on the second day of play or past the dinner break, or whenever it was. Even if we have no chance of winning the championship, we want to hang in. It's a real mistake to give up hope and think, This is my last shot. Your last shot is your last chip. Every time someone is eliminated, it's a benefit to you. The point is to survive."

Johnny Chan said much the same, but from a different point of view. Chan is small and trim and compact, with a heart-shaped face and eyes like stone. He won the World Championship twice, in 1987 and 1988, and by 1994 he had become the first player to bring his total earnings in the World Series to more than two million dollars—to $2,038,544, to be precise. Chan tends to talk in imperatives, a style that goes with his commanding presence, and he reacts to amateurs like a great white shark reacts to blood: "No-limit is a game to trap people," he told me one afternoon when he was taking a break from the monster game at table 61. "When you find a weak player, try to get everyone else out. Now it's between you and the weak player. Now you need to trap him, make him lose something. You don't have a hand—who cares? Bluff him out. He's weak. Make a play. When you sit down, you look around the table and see how many weak players there are. Who is the

⊗ opposite page: Jack Binion, longtime president of Binion's Horseshoe, was the driving force behind the World Series of Poker.

weakest? That's the one you go for. You try to avoid the good players until you get to the final table. That's what you've got to do to win."

"Sometimes weak players get lucky and fluke their way through," I said hopefully.

"It happens. If the best players won every time it would be very boring. There would be no tournament. Everybody has the opportunity to win. If I have two aces and a weak player has two queens, and at the end he catches a queen, what am I going to do? So he wins the money, OK?"

"But suppose it was the other way around: you have the queens, he has the aces?"

"That happens, too. But I try not to go broke with two queens. That's the difference between the good player and the weak player. If you don't have the nuts you shouldn't put all your money in."

When Studley talked about not giving up hope, he made me understand how hopeless my position was at this level of poker. Chan's staccato commands deepened my gloom. So did Artie Cobb, but after I talked to him one evening over dinner in the Sombrero Room, at least I began to understand the measure of the difference between the small fry and the great whites.

Cobb has ginger hair, a big belly, a mournful face, and a taste for funny hats. He is a talented poker player, who has won three tournaments in the World Series, but he is not up there with the champions and has thought deeply about why this is so. "There are a lot of fine players out there, but the great player always has that little edge on them," he said. "The player who is not great has tendencies he always falls into when he has a good hand, a mediocre hand, or a weak hand. The great players can spot them easily. They read the table like a walking computer. They understand when they have to gamble more and when they have to gamble less. The average player

doesn't always understand that. When the game starts, everyone has the same number of chips. The favorites are favorites because they know what they have to do to win the tournament. They can't stay idle and hope they're going to double-up their stack along the way. They try to increase it a little bit at every limit, sometimes even with marginal hands most people don't want to play, like an ace with a doubtful kicker. I remember an extraordinary hand played by Stu Ungar and Doyle Brunson. Both of them had ace-queen in the hole, and Gabe Kaplan, the actor, was there with king-jack. The flop was ace, ace, king. Stuey made a small bet on the flop and the others called. The next card was a three. Stuey came out betting, Gabe folded, and Doyle just moved all in. It was a huge bet, and if Stuey called and won, Doyle would have been out of the tournament. Each of them knew the other had an ace, so it was down to the kicker. An amateur might have thought an ace was good enough or that Doyle would only move all in with a full house—with ace-king or ace-trey in the hole. But somehow Stuey sensed that Doyle was making a play. He thought a long time, and if he had had less than ace-queen he might have folded. It was possible that Doyle had ace-jack, but that was unlikely, knowing how well he plays. So Stuey figured they must have the same hand, ace-queen. He called, and they split the pot. And that's a mind-set only great players get into. That's the deep part of the game which the average player has no concept of."

I played in three events in the World Series—the $1,500-buy-in Texas hold 'em (pot limit), the $2,500-buy-in Texas hold 'em (no limit), and the $10,000-buy-in World Championship itself—and each was grimmer than the last. That made good sense to me, since the prize money shared out among the finalists grew steadily more serious in each event:

⊗ opposite page: Johnny Chan, World Champion of 1987 and 1988, was the first player whose World Series earnings topped two million dollars.

$370,500 in the $1,500 tournament, $550,000 in the $2,500 game, and a staggering $2,680,000 in the World Championship. It also made sense that I played less freely as the grandeur of the occasion increased. But while the World Series was in progress, I was also playing in cash games, and what didn't make sense was how my play in them was like a mirror image of the way I played in the tournaments. Hold 'em is, among other things, a game of calculated aggression: if your cards are good enough for you to call a bet, they are good enough to raise with. According to Don Williams, a small, bearded, fast-talking, and successful professional, "When you're betting, you've got two chances of winning: you can take the pot there and then, or you can have the best hand. When you're calling a bet, you've only got one chance: you've got to have the best hand. But you don't win tournaments just by showing the best hand." I followed his advice in the cash games and did very well; whenever I had bet before the flop I bet again after it, if the other players checked, even when the exposed cards had not helped my hand. More often than not, the original callers meekly folded, and I took the money. But I only played in the modest pot-limit cash games, with other amateurs and small-time professionals. The heavy hitters were busy elsewhere.

Even so, the tournaments started encouragingly for me. The morning after I arrived in Vegas, I played three $165 satellites for a place in the $1,500-pot-limit Texas hold 'em event and won the third. By the time the last satellite finished, the tournament was beginning (forty-five minutes late), so I had no time to brood. There wasn't even much to brood about. I've played for those stakes before, so the money didn't scare me. Nor did the players; although most of the poker stars were playing, none of them came to the tables I was at. And if they had, I would probably not have noticed; I was in the no-man's-land of jet lag

compounded by a fitful night's sleep and was playing on automatic pilot. That was OK, too, because pot-limit hold 'em, where you may never bet more than is already in the pot, is the type of poker I play back home in London. It is my game, and to prove it I'd waltzed through a satellite to get there. In other words, Las Vegas hadn't yet gotten to me. By the time the game was about four hours old and around 80 of the original 247 starters were left, I had tripled my original stack and was beginning to think that maybe I might make it to the final table. At that point, hubris struck, I made a foolish mistake, and was gone ten minutes later. I blamed it on jet lag.

I also got into the $2,500 (no-limit) hold 'em event through a satellite—or rather, by surviving in a number of satellites until only two or three players were left, and then dividing the spoils. (Satellites are played with special tournament chips that have no value outside the game; the winner is also paid in special gray chips, similar to the casino's $1 chips, though even more battered and unprepossessing; each is worth $500.) It took me just over a week of inter-mittent satellite play to rustle up enough chips for the $2,500 event. By that time I was fully tuned in to Vegas, its hierarchies, its insane values, and to the seriousness of what I was getting into.

The event was played on the last Friday of the World Series and was a dress rehearsal for the big one, which was scheduled to begin on the following Monday. There were 220 entries, including most of the stars, and enough prize money to solve all my problems. I responded to the occasion by playing the kind of poker I used to play in my ignorant youth when I imagined the game had something to do with gambling. In no-limit hold 'em, where any mistake can be terminal, this was lunacy, but it was brought on by dumb luck. As soon as the game began, I was bombarded with good cards—with big pairs, with aces and high kickers of the same suit—until I began to think I could do no wrong. Psychoanalysts call this state of mind "mania"; the poker pros describe it more vividly: "He wanted to give his money away," they say, "but the cards wouldn't let him." I walked on water for less than an hour, then made two disgraceful calls, and sank ignominiously. I scuttered back upstairs with my head down, in case I met anyone I knew. Even when the door of my room was locked behind me, I was too ashamed to brush my hair because it meant seeing my face in the mirror.

The weekend before the World Championship, Binion's Horseshoe was like a pressure cooker with the heat turned up full beneath it. The casino was packed with gawking spectators, the poker pits swarmed with TV crews, with self-important people flashing press cards and asking dumb questions, with players short of funds working the crowd, trying to hustle deals. In the cash games tempers frayed: one player threw his cards at the dealer after a bad beat; a white-bearded old man started a shouting match with a thin-lipped Greek thirty years his junior, invited him outside to settle the matter, then marched off, muttering obscenities. There was a final feeding frenzy in the $1,000 satellites. People were buying in, losing, buying in again, as though a thousand dollars truly were no more than a dime. Behind them, a group of professionals lounged against the rail like vultures in a tree, waiting to pick off an easy satellite to save themselves the ten-grand entry fee on Monday. The air conditioning seemed unable to cope, the voices on the intercom never let up, the sheer predatoriness was battering. I ground back some money and pride in a cash game and went to bed early.

The morning of the big day was chilly and overcast. A brisk wind was blowing, and I had the pool to myself. Around 12:30, I wandered down to the casino. Although crowds were gathering around the tournament area and journalists bustled about, the frenzy of the last few days was over. The players stood around in little groups, talking in subdued voices, eyeing the opposition. Off to one side, Jack McClelland, the tournament coordinator, sat at a table drawing the seat numbers and droning them out on the intercom. The big board behind him had space for 240 names, but that was not enough. Because of the satellites and the fact that this was the silver anniversary of the World Series, 268 hopefuls, a record, had signed up for the World Championship. The sight of my own name, at number 182, up there with all those champions whom I had watched for years from a safe distance, should have been exhilarating. Instead, it filled me with gloom.

There were formalities to go through before the action started: a tribute to the late Telly Savalas, who competed twelve times in the big event; "Gentleman" Jack Keller, the 1984 World Champion, was inducted into the Poker Hall of Fame; Jack Binion made a brief opening speech. Then we all dispersed to our appointed seats. Mine was seat 1 at table 56; at $10,000, it was the most expensive seat I had ever sat on. Next to me was Billy Baxter, a famous high-roller and one of the great deuce-to-the-seven players. Jack Keller was in seat 6. Ken Flaton, another expert, was in seat 8. As I watched them amble up, I remembered the old proverb, "Beware of what you wish for; you may get it."

Finally, the chatter subsided, and Jack McClelland gave the starting orders: "Dealers, shuffle up and deal."

Mick Cooke, an Englishman I know, once made it to the final table. "In the early stages, I came in with nothing lower than a pair of jacks," he said later. Two jacks are strong enough to call with, and easy to throw away. A pair of queens is a trickier hand to play; I was dealt them four times—twice in the first fifteen minutes—and in the end they were my undoing. But my first mistake occurred an hour or so into the game. I was dealt an eight and seven of diamonds when I was in the big blind. There were two or three callers, but no raise. The dealer thumped the table, burned (discarded) the top card, and dealt six, nine, ten. The seven and eight in my hand gave me a straight. It was an almost perfect flop, except that the exposed nine and ten were both hearts. I checked, in the hope of trapping someone, and a young woman named Barbara Samuelson came out betting. She was tall and rangy, with a mannish figure, a small face and large hands, and her style of play was fearless and aggressive. I should have moved all in immediately to shut her out, but greed overcame me; I wanted more of her chips. So I raised a paltry thousand, and she called. The next card was bad for me: the queen of hearts, making a possible flush and a higher straight. When I checked, she checked. The last card was a king, and this time she bet strongly. I should have folded—any good player would have folded—but I was in love with my puny straight, so I made a crying call. She had a pair of jacks in the hole and had made a higher straight than mine. (Samuelson eventually placed tenth—at that time the highest-ever finish by a woman in this event.)

At least I wasn't the only one making mistakes. Within two hours, three former World Champions had gone. "Gentleman" Jack Keller slow-played a pair of aces, moved all in when a king and a ten flopped, and was called instantly by Billy Baxter, who had king-ten in the hole. Minutes later, Stu Ungar, who won the title in 1980 and 1981, and was to win it again in 1997, stalked past, looking furious. Phil Hellmuth Jr., winner in 1989, followed. "I had two aces, but I ran into a pair of tens," he said. Billy Baxter watched them go. "I'll tell you one thing," he said contentedly. "They sure knocked some whales out of this already."

Baxter promptly got into a raising battle with a friend of his who had moved into Keller's seat. When it ended, both had all their chips in the center and both had pairs of aces. Much jocular relief on both sides.

At 3:45 there was a ten-minute break. As we settled again around the table, Baxter and his pal were chatting together about hold 'em. "Not my pond," Baxter was saying.

"Hell, man, you just busted a guy in the Hall of Fame."

"That just shows you I'm not long for this world."

For the next hour and a half, my chips bled away in antes while I folded unplayable hands. Then, for the fourth time, I was dealt two queens. I bet a thousand, and Baxter instantly reraised another thousand. Maybe I should have moved all in to shut him out. But he had position over me and a massive amount of chips. So I just called. The flop was king, seven, deuce. When I checked and he bet two thousand, I knew what his hole cards were: an ace and a king. With anything stronger, he would have checked to trap me; with less, he would have checked for fear of being trapped. My only hope was to catch one of the two queens remaining in the deck or to bluff him. I suppose I should have folded there and then and kept my last two grand for a better spot. But the antes were eating me up, and that pair of queens in my hand seemed like a mountain after the lowly cards I'd been seeing. I thought and thought, then called, hoping my long pause might have puzzled him. The next card was another deuce. That was my chance. I pushed in what was left of my stack and said, "Come on, Billy, let's gamble." He looked at me slit-eyed and hesitated. "You got a deuce?" he asked. And for a moment I thought I'd bluffed him out. But the pot was large and the bet was small, so he called. The last card was a jack. Without waiting, he turned over the ace-king I knew he had.

⊗ opposite page: Stu "The Kid" Ungar, World Champion of 1980, 1981, and 1997.

When Adlai Stevenson lost to Eisenhower in 1952, he said that he was too old to cry, but it hurt too much to laugh. I understood how he felt. I had been preparing for this day for fifteen months, and when it came I blew it. I had made the classic mistake of a newcomer to the big league: I played what the pros call "tight-weak"—afraid to bet without the stone-cold nuts and easily scared out. But at this level players can smell your fear, and they run all over you. I couldn't even complain about bad beats. On the contrary, I knew justice had been done. I am a good pot limit player, but in pot limit you can make a big enough bet to bluff an opponent out without putting your whole stack in jeopardy. No limit is different. You get very few chances, and the smallest mistake can destroy you. I had failed to take the chances I'd been offered, and ended by making a big mistake.

The first person I saw when I left the table was an Englishman who knows all the odds. "At least you were beaten with the best hand," he said consolingly. "Two queens are a fifty-five to forty-five favorite over ace-king off-suit."

A few minutes later, as though to prove his point, I watched a replay of the identical hand at an adjacent table: someone bet with ace-king off-suit, then called a massive all in reraise by a guy holding a pair of queens. But this time the first card to be flopped was a queen, giving the raiser three queens and making him chip leader of the tournament at that point.

At breakfast the next morning, I saw Herb Bronstein, who was considered a strong contender for the title. He, too, looked stricken. "Yeah, I'm an also-ran," he said. "You wait a whole year for your chance and then it's gone."

"I've been waiting all my life," I answered.

When I called my wife in London with the news, she burst into tears.

The World Championship is a four-day event and, like the other also-rans, I could not bring myself to watch it with any interest until the last day, when the field had been reduced to six and show biz took over. The final table was set up, as though for a prize-fight, in a fenced-off square, its entrances blocked by security guards. Around the table was a cordon sanitaire for the television crews and press photographers. Behind it, and flanked by two big TV screens, was a dais on which the players were interviewed as they were eliminated from the game. Hanging all around were banners inscribed "World Series of Poker/Binion's Horseshoe/Silver Anniversary." There were two blocks of reserved seats—one for the players, the other for the press—but no matter how close you sat all you could see was a slumped back, a profile, a foot tapping secretly below the table. The things that really mattered—the cards, the facial expressions, the size of the bets and the manner in which they were made, the dealers' deft, eloquent fingers as they handled the cards—could only be seen fleetingly on the TV monitors.

In best prizefight style, there was a weigh-in before the start, so that the winner's weight in silver would be ready at the end. By 10:25 the ceremonies were over. For the last time, Jack McClelland called,

⊗ top: A 1905 illustration of a gentlemen's game.

⊗ opposite page: Stu Ungar, left, and Doyle Brunson, right, go head-to-head at the final table of the World Series, 1980.

"Shuffle up and deal," and the cards were spun out. Within two and a half hours, three finalists had been eliminated, two of them when they moved all in against players holding ace-queen, and a queen came on the flop. Each time the queen was dealt, I thought, Where were you when I needed you?

Then the action froze. The chip leader was Hugh Vincent, a scrawny, bespectacled, chain-smoking amateur, with a goatee, a cheap white buttoned shirt, and a blue cap. He had begun the day with almost $1,500,000 in chips—more than half the money in play—and he used his muscle to harry the other players, pushing his luck, living on the edge, playing brilliantly by the seat of his pants. Close behind him was Russ Hamilton, a Las Vegas professional. He weighed in at 330 pounds, and when he climbed on the scales before the start, they ran out of silver ingots. He had pale hair, a ghost of a beard, and sharp, calculating blue eyes. At the table, he was a thoughtful and forbidding presence, biding his time, making no mistakes. He sat for what seemed hours without stirring; only his eyes moved, missing nothing. A long way behind came John Spadavecchia, a Miami businessman

who looked as if he had just walked out of a Scorsese movie: a creased face with a lot of mileage on it, dark hair, dark shirt, gold watch, gold bracelet, gold ring.

The 1994 World Series had already broken all sorts of records, including the total number of entrants into all the events (3,832) and the total prize money distributed ($9,969,500). In the World Championship event, more records went: it had the largest entry (268), the highest-placed woman player (Barbara Samuelson), the largest single pot ($1,980,000), and, in the closing stages, the biggest-ever blind bets ($25,000 and $50,000). The other record broken was the three-handed marathon that ended the game: more than five hours passed without a player being eliminated, while Spadavecchia tried to claw his way back to level terms and Vincent leaked his money away, little by little, to Hamilton.

Spadavecchia went, finally, at 6:25. Five minutes later, Hamilton was dealt a pair of queens, saw a third queen appear on the flop, and trapped Vincent into the largest pot in the history of the event. Ten minutes later, it was over. Russ Hamilton had the title, $1,000,000 of prize money, $28,512 in silver ingots,

the winner's gold bracelet, and the honor of having his picture up on the wall of the poker room along with all the other greats.

That evening, I had dinner with my old friend and fellow poker player, Tony Holden. Afterwards, we wandered back to the tournament area to find a game. But there was no tournament area. The tables had gone, the players had gone. All that was left was a cleaning man wearily vacuuming an empty stretch of leaf-patterned carpet. It looked desolate.

We stood there for a while in silence. Then I said, "Why do they always get the queen when they need it and we don't?"

"That's the mystery of life and poker," Tony said. "I guess the answer is they invented the game, so they deserve it."

GLOSSARY *of* POKER TERMS

A

ACE-HIGH > A five-card hand containing an ace but no pair; beats a king-high, but loses to any pair or higher hand.

ACES UP > Two pairs, one of which is aces.

ACTION > Bets and raises.

ADVERTISE > To make a bluff with the deliberate intention of being exposed as a "loose" player.

ALL IN > To bet all the chips you have left.

ANTE > A compulsory stake before the deal.

ANTE UP > A dealer's request for antes to be paid.

B

BACK TO BACK > *See* Wired.

BACK DOOR > To make a hand you were not originally drawing to.

BAD BEAT > To lose a pot against heavy odds, as when a strong hand is beaten by a lucky underdog.

BELLY-BUSTER STRAIGHT > An inside straight.

BET INTO > To take the initiative and bet instead of checking to a player who bet strongly on the previous round.

BET THE POT > To bet the total value of money in the pot.

BICYCLE > The lowest possible hand in low ball, A-2-3-4-5. *See* Wheel.

BIG BLIND > In hold 'em and Omaha, the largest compulsory ante, usually made by the player to the dealer's left.

BIG SLICK > In hold 'em, Ace-King, a strong starting hand.

BLANK > In hold 'em, a card on Fourth or Fifth Street that is of no value to the player's hand.

BLIND (1) > The compulsory bet or bets to the dealer's left.

BLIND (2) > To check or bet without looking at your hole cards.

BLOW BACK > To lose back most or all of one's profits.

BOARD > The five communal or community cards in a hold 'em or Omaha game; or the "up" cards in a game of stud.

BOBTAIL > *See* Open-ended Straight.

BOSS > The strongest hand at that stage, as in "boss trips."

BOTTOM PAIR > In hold 'em, a pair with the lowest card on the flop; e.g., if you hold Ah-7h and the flop is K-J-7, you have flopped the bottom pair.

BRING IT IN FOR > To make the first optional bet.

BUCK > Originally, a clasp knife with a buckhorn handle that was passed around the table to indicate who was dealing. Hence the phrase "the buck stops here." *See* Button.

BULLET > An ace.

BUMP > To raise.

BURN > To discard the top card, facedown, before dealing out the cards (to prevent cheating); or to set aside a card which has been inadvertently revealed.

BUST > A worthless hand that has failed to improve as the player hoped.

BUST A PLAYER > To deprive a player of all his chips; in tournament play, to eliminate him.

BUSTED > Broke, or tapped.

BUSTED FLUSH > A four-flush that failed to fill up.

BUSTED OUT, BE BUSTED OUT > To be eliminated from a tournament by losing all your chips.

BUTTON > A plastic disk used by a professional dealer to indicate which player is notionally dealing the hand and should therefore receive the last card. Also used to refer to the player who is "on the button." *See* Buck.

BUY-IN > The minimum amount of money required to sit down in a particular game.

BY ME > A popular (usually amateur) alternative to "check" or "fold."

C

CALIFORNIA or **ACE-TO-THE-FIVE LOW BALL** > A form of low ball in which the ace counts low, straights and flushes do not count against you, and the best possible hand is A-2-3-4-5. *See* Wheel.

CALL > To match, rather than raise, the previous bet.

CALLING STATION > A weak or passive player who invariably calls and is therefore hard to bluff out.

CARDS SPEAK > A form of hi-lo poker in which there is no declaration before the showdown.

CASE CARD > The last card of a denomination or suit, when the rest have been dealt, as in "the case ace."

CASH IN or **CASH OUT** > To leave a game and convert one's chips to cash.

CATCH > To "pull" the card you want.

CHASE > To stay in against a stronger hand in the hope of outdrawing it.

CHECK (1) > Not to bet, reserving the right to call or raise if another player bets.

CHECK (2) > Another name for a poker chip.

CHECK BLIND or **CHECK IN THE DARK** > To check your hand without looking at it.

CHECK-RAISE > To check and then raise when the betting gets back to you. *See* Sandbag.

CINCH HAND > A hand that cannot be beaten. *See* Nuts.

COFFEE HOUSING > Attempting to mislead or confuse opponents by devious speech or behavior.

COLD > A bad streak, as in, "My cards have gone cold."

COLD CALL > To call a bet and a raise when you have not yet invested any money in the pot.

COLD DECK > A deck of cards "fixed" in advance by a cheat.

COME > To play an as yet worthless hand in the hope of improving it, as in playing "on the come."

COMPLETE HAND > *See* Made Hand.

CONNECTORS > In hold 'em, a starting hand in which the two cards are one apart in rank, e.g., 7-8 or J-Q.

COWBOY > Slang for king.

CRIPPLE THE DECK > In hold 'em, to hold most or all of the cards the other players might want, e.g., a pair of queens when there are two queens on the flop.

CRYING CALL > To call a bet unwillingly, afraid that you are beaten.

CUT IT UP > To divide, or split, the pot after a tie.

CUT THE POT > To take chips from the pot on behalf of the house. *See* Rake.

D

DEAD > A hand or card that is no longer legally playable due to some irregularity.

DEALER'S CHOICE > A game in which each dealer, in turn, chooses the type of poker to be played.

DECLARATION > In hi-lo poker, declaring by the use of coins or chips, whether one is aiming to win the high or the low end of the pot, or both.

DEUCE > A two, the lowest-ranking card in high poker.

DEUCE-TO-THE-SEVEN (or KANSAS CITY) LOW BALL > A form of low ball in which the best hand is 2-3-4-5-7. Ace is always a high card and straights and flushes count against you.

DOG > Short for "underdog," opposite of "favorite."

DOOR CARD > The first up card in a stud game.

DOWN CARDS > The hole cards.

DOWN TO THE GREEN > Having all your chips in the pot, leaving only the green baize tabletop in front of you. *See* All In.

DRAWING DEAD > Drawing to a hand that cannot win even if you make it.

DRAW OUT > To win a hand on the last card or cards, after staying with an inferior hand. *See* Back Door.

DRIVER'S SEAT (IN THE) > Said of a player who is making all the betting and thus appears to hold the strongest hand.

DROP > To fold.

F

FAMILY POT > A pot in which all the players call before the flop.

FIFTH STREET > In hold 'em and Omaha, the fifth communal card to be exposed; also known as "the river."

FILL, FILL UP > To "pull" the card you are seeking.

FLAT CALL > To call a bet without raising.

FLOORMAN > A card room supervisor; the ultimate arbiter of disputes.

FLOP > In hold 'em and Omaha, the first three communal or community cards to be dealt faceup in the center of the table.

FLOP A SET > In hold 'em and Omaha, when you hold a pair in the hole and one of the three community cards is of the same rank.

FLUSH > Five cards of the same suit; ranks above a straight and below a full house.

FOLD > To withdraw from, or give up, the hand.

FOUR FLUSH > Four cards of the same suit, requiring a fifth to become a flush.

FOUR OF A KIND or **QUADS** > Four cards of the same denomination. Beats a full house; can be beaten only by a straight flush.

FREE CARD or **RIDE** > To stay in a hand without being forced to bet.

FREE ROLL > When two players are tied before the final cards are dealt, the one whose hand can improve is said to be on a free roll.

FREEZE OUT > A game, usually a tournament, in which all players buy in once only, for the same amount of chips, and play until one player has won all the chips.

FULL HOUSE > A hand containing trips and a pair. Between two full houses, the higher trips win. Beats straights and flushes; loses to four of a kind.

G

GRAVEYARD > The predawn shift in a Las Vegas casino.

GUTSHOT > The card needed to fill an inside straight.

H

HEADS-UP, HEAD-TO-HEAD > A game between just two players, often the climax of a tournament.

HIGH ROLLER > One who gambles for large sums of money.

HIGH-LOW, HI-LO > A species of poker in which the highest and the lowest hands share the pot.

HIT > To obtain the card you are seeking.

HOLE CARDS > The cards dealt facedown which only the player can see, a.k.a. Pocket.

HOT > Said of a player on a winning streak.

HOUSE > A full house.

I

IGNORANT END > The low end of a straight.

IMPROVE > To pull a card or cards that better one's hand.

IN > A player is "in" if he has called all bets.

IN THE DARK > To be in the dark is to check or bet blind, without looking at your cards.

INSIDE STRAIGHT > Four cards requiring (an unlikely) one in the middle to fill a straight, viz. 5-6-7-9, a.k.a. Belly Buster; *see* open-ended straight.

K

KIBITZER > A nonplaying spectator, or railbird.

KICK IT > To raise.

KICKER > The subsidiary or "side" card to a more powerful card or cards.

KNAVE > A jack.

KNOCK > *See* Rap.

L

LADY > A queen.

LAY DOWN > To reveal one's hand in a showdown.

LIMIT POKER > A game with fixed betting intervals, e.g, $10–$20, $20–$40.

LIMP IN > To call a bet. *See* Flat Call.

LITTLE BLIND > *See* Small Blind.

LIVE BLIND > A forced bet put in before the deal but giving the player the option to raise when the action gets back to him.

LIVE CARD > A card that has not been dealt or seen.

LIVE ONE > An inexperienced, bad, or loose player; a sucker who has money to lose.

LOCK > A hand that cannot lose. *See* Cinch *and* Nuts.

LOOK > To call or see the final bet.

LOOSE > Liberal play, usually in defiance of the odds.

LOW BALL > A form of poker in which the lowest hand wins.

M

MADE HAND > A perfect hand which cannot be improved, e.g., a straight, flush, full house, or better. *See* Pat Hand.

MAKE (THE DECK) > To shuffle.

MARK > A sucker.

MARKER > An IOU.

MECHANIC > A card cheat who manipulates the deck.

MONEY MANAGEMENT > The art of controlling your bankroll in order to stay in the game and/or not to commit chips unnecessarily to the pot.

MOVE IN > To bet all your chips.

MUCK > The discard pile, in which all cards are dead.

N

NO LIMIT > A game in which a player may bet any amount of the chips he has on the table, regardless of the size of the pot.

NUT FLUSH > The best available flush.

NUTS > The best, unbeatable hand at any stage of a game, a.k.a. "the stone-cold nuts."

O

OFF-SUIT > Cards of different suits.

OMAHA > A four-card variation of hold 'em, in which you *must* use two of the cards in your hand.

ON TILT > When a player starts playing badly, usually after losing one or two big pots.

OPEN > To make the first bet.

OPEN-ENDED STRAIGHT > Four consecutive cards requiring one at either end to make a straight, viz. 5-6-7-8; also known as a two-way straight, or a "bobtail."

OUTDRAW > *See* Draw Out.

OUTS > The cards that would turn a losing hand into a winner.

OVERCARDS > In hold 'em, cards higher than the flop cards, played in hope of catching a higher pair.

OVERPAIR > In hold 'em, a pocket pair higher than any card on the flop.

P

PAINT > Any "picture" or court card.

PAIR > Two cards of the same denomination.

PASS > To fold; occasionally (wrongly) used for check.

PAT HAND > A hand that is complete or made as dealt.

PICTURE CARD > King, queen, or jack, also known as court card, face card, or paint.

PIP > The suit symbols on a noncourt card, indicating its rank.

PLAY BACK (AT) > To reraise.

PLAY BEHIND > When a player declares (usually before the beginning of a hand) that he is playing for more money than he has on the table.

PLAY OVER > To occupy a seat that is temporarily vacant.

PLAY THE BOARD > In hold 'em, to show down a hand that cannot beat the hand made by the five community cards.

POCKET (IN THE) > The cards only you can see, a.k.a. hole.

POSITION > Your seat in relation to the dealer, and thus your place in the betting order; an important tactical consideration.

POT > The chips at stake in the center of the table.

POT LIMIT > A game in which the maximum bet is the total amount of money in the pot.

POT ODDS > The amount of money in the pot compared to the amount you must contribute to continue playing, i.e., the price the pot is offering you when you call a bet.

PUT DOWN > To fold.

Q

QUADS > *See* Four of a Kind.

R

RAGS > Low, bad, or unconnected cards.

RAILBIRD > A nonplaying spectator or kibitzer.

RAISE > To call and increase the previous bet.

RAKE > Chips taken from the pot by the dealer on behalf of the house.

RAP > To "knock" the table, to indicate a check.

RAZZ > Seven-card stud for low. Also a form of draw low ball.

READ > To try to figure out the cards your opponent is holding.

REBUY > To start again, for an additional entry fee, in tournament play (when permitted).

RERAISE > To raise a raiser.

REPRESENT > To bet in a way that suggests you are holding a (usually strong) hand that you do not in fact have.

RIFFLE > To shuffle the deck, or to fidget with your chips.

RIVER > In hold 'em and Omaha, the fifth and final communal card to be exposed.

ROCK > An ultratight and not very creative player, who usually raises only with the nuts.

ROYAL STRAIGHT FLUSH > A-K-Q-J-10 of the same suit. The best possible poker hand in all but wild-card games.

RUN (1) > Synonym for a straight.

RUN (2) > A run of good cards. *See* Rush *and* Streak.

RUNNING BAD > On a losing streak.

RUNNING GOOD > On a winning streak.

RUSH > A succession of good cards. A player "on a rush" may well "play his rush," i.e., play an indifferent hand because he's feeling lucky, and might win against the odds. *See* Run *and* Streak.

S

SANDBAG > To check a strong hand with the intention of raising.

SATELLITE > A small-stakes tournament whose winner obtains cheap entry into a bigger tournament.

SCHOOL > Collective noun for the players in a regular game.

SECOND PAIR > In hold 'em, a pair made by one of your hole cards with the second highest card on the board.

SEE > To call.

SET > Three of a kind, or trips.

SET YOU IN > To bet as much as your opponent has left in front of him.

SHILL > A card-room employee who plays with house money to make up a game.

SHORT STACK > A small number of chips compared to those in front of other players.

SHOWDOWN > The final revealing of the hole cards, after betting has ceased.

SHY > To owe money to the pot.

SIDE CARD > *See* Kicker.

SIDE POT > A separate pot contested by other players when one player is all in.

SLOW PLAY > To play a strong hand weakly in the hope of tempting players with worse hands into the pot.

SMALL BLIND > In hold 'em, the smaller of the two antes, compulsory to the player on the dealer's left.

SPLIT > A tie, or standoff, usually when two or more players have hands of equal value, though occasionally a split can be agreed between two players before the showdown.

SQUEEZE > In draw poker, to look slowly at your hole cards in order to worry your opponents (or yourself) and heighten the drama.

STAND PAT > To decline an opportunity to draw cards.

STAY > To remain in a hand with a call rather than a raise.

STEAL > A bluff in late position in the hope of "stealing" the pot when there has been no action.

STEAMING > Playing badly and wildly. *See* On Tilt.

STRADDLE > To make an extra "blind" raise before the deal.

STRAIGHT > Five consecutively ranked cards, not of the same suit. Beats trips, but loses to a flush and above.

STRAIGHT FLUSH > Five consecutive cards of the same suit. Beats everything but a higher straight flush.

STREAK > A run of good (or bad) cards. *See* Run *and* Rush.

STRING BET > An illegal bet (or, more usually, a raise) in which a player does not put all the necessary chips in the pot at once. Unless he has verbally declared his bet before raising, he can be forced to withdraw it and simply call.

STUCK > Slang for losing.

STUD > Any form of poker in which the first card or cards are dealt facedown, or in the hole, followed by several open or "up" cards.

SUITED > Cards of the same suit, as in "A-K suited."

SWEETEN (THE POT) > To raise.

T

TABLE STAKES > A poker game in which a player cannot bet more than the money he has on the table.

TAP CITY > To be broke.

TAP OUT > To bet all one's chips or go broke.

TELL > A give-away mannerism or nervous habit by which an opponent reveals the strength or otherwise of his hand; possibly from *telltale.*

THREE FLUSH > Three cards of the same suit.

THREE OF A KIND > Three cards of the same denomination; beats two pairs but loses to a straight or above, a.k.a. Set, Triplets or Trips.

TIGHT > A conservative player who plays only strong hands. *See* Rock.

TOKE > A tip to the dealer (illegal in Britain).

TOP PAIR > In hold 'em, a pair made by one of your hole cards with the highest card on the board.

TREY > A three.

TRIPLETS or **TRIPS** > *See* Three of a Kind *and* Set.

TURN > In hold 'em and Omaha, the fourth communal card to be dealt, a.k.a. Fourth Street.

TWO PAIRS > A hand containing two pairs plus a kicker beats a pair but loses to trips or above.

U

UNDER-BET > To make a small bet, usually in the hope of enticing a raise.

UNDERDOG > *See* Dog.

UNDERRAISE > To raise less than the previous bet, allowed only if a player is going all in.

UNDER THE GUN > The first player to bet.

UP CARD > An "open," or exposed, card in stud poker.

W

WHEEL > The lowest hand in low ball, A-2-3-4-5, a.k.a. Bicycle.

WHIPSAW > To raise before, and after, a caller who is caught in the middle.

WILD CARD > Any card designated as a joker.

WIRED > A pair dealt in the first two cards, as in "aces wired," a.k.a. Back to Back.

INDEX

CREDITS

GRATEFUL ACKNOWLEDGMENT IS MADE FOR THE FOLLOWING:

From *The Education of a Poker Player,* by Herbert O. Yardley. Copyright ©1957, copyright renewed by Herbert O. Yardley. Reprinted with permission of Orloff Press. In the United Kingdom, reprinted by permission of Oldcastle Books Ltd.

From *Little Book of Poker,* by David Spanier. Copyright ©2000 by David Spanier. Reprinted with permission of Huntington Press. In the United Kingdom, reprinted with the permission of Oldcastle Books Ltd.

Excerpt from *Double Down: Reflections on Gambling and Loss,* by Frederick and Steven Barthelme. Copyright ©1999 by Frederick and Steven Barthelme. Reprinted with permission of Houghton Mifflin Company. In the United Kingdom, reprinted with the permission of The Wylie Agency, Inc.

From *Big Deal,* by Anthony Holden. Copyright ©1990 by Anthony Holden Ltd. Used by permission of Viking Penguin, a division of Penguin Group (USA). In the United Kindgdom, reproduced with permission of the author c/o Rogers, Coleridge, & White Ltd., 20 Powis Mews, London W11 1JN.

From *From Here to Eternity,* by James Jones. Copyright ©1951 by James Jones. Copyright renewed 1979 by Gloria Jones, James Anthony Phillipe Jones and Kaylie Anne Jones. Used by permission of Dell Publishing, a division of Random House, Inc.

From *Total Poker*, by David Spanier. Copyright ©1977 by David Spanier. Reprinted by permission of Oldcastle Books Ltd.

PICTURE CREDITS

Ulvis Alberts, photographer, pages: 16, 23, 24, 43, 45, 49, 52, 54, 57, 61, 63, 65, 91, 104, 109, 115, 117.

Al Alvarez, page: 31.

Buffalo Bill Historical Center, page: 88.

Everett Collection, pages: 14, 73, 79, 80, 81, 85, 93.

Jim Faller, pages: 11, 12, 21, 64, 77 top, 77 bottom, 87, 89 left, 89 right, 102 left, 102 right, 103 left, 103 right, 116.

Larry Grossman, pages: 42, 53, 62, 97, 110.

Robert Limacher, pages: 25 left, 25 right, 26 top, 26 bottom, 35 top, 35 bottom, 38, 56, 64 left, 64 right, 69 three images, 71, 78, 128 top, 128 bottom.

Nevada State Museum, pages: 95, 99.

Underwood Archives, pages: 26, 40, 59, 74 left, 74 right.

Byron Walker, pages: 9, 10 left, 10 right, 18, 19 top, 19 bottom, 28, 33 top, 33 bottom, 36 left, 36 right, 39 left, 39 bottom, 41, 44, 47, 50, 106.

⊗ Every effort has been made to trace accurate ownership of copyrighted text and visual material used in this book. Errors or omissions will be corrected in subsequent editions, provided notification is sent to the publisher.

"TRUST EVERYONE BUT ALWAYS CUT THE CARDS."

Benny Binion